HAPPY AS A
DANE

HAPPY AS A
DANE

10 Secrets of the Happiest People
in the World

MALENE RYDAHL

W. W. NORTON & COMPANY

Independent Publishers Since 1923

New York | London

For information about permission to reproduce selections from
this book, write to Permissions, W. W. Norton & Company, Inc.,
500 Fifth Avenue, New York, NY 10110

For information about special discounts for bulk purchases,
please contact W. W. Norton Special Sales at
specialsales@wwnorton.com or 800-233-4830

Manufacturing by Quad Graphics
Book design by Chris Welch
Production manager: Lauren Abbate

ISBN: 978-0-393-60892-2 (pbk.)

W. W. Norton & Company, Inc.
500 Fifth Avenue, New York, N.Y. 10110
www.wwnorton.com

W. W. Norton & Company Ltd.
15 Carlisle Street, London W1D 3BS

2 3 4 5 6 7 8 9 0

For the freedom to be true to yourself
and the courage to pursue
a happy life with purpose

12. 12.

Contents

CONTENTS

ONCE UPON A TIME . . .

Once upon a time there was a young Danish
woman who decided to write a book
about happiness.

While writing it, she went on vacation to the south of France. She was invited to an elegant dinner party in a stunning house overlooking the sea. The guests were beautiful and everything was perfect, just like a dream. For predinner drinks they were offered fine vintages of champagne and wine, and every exotic cocktail you could imagine. They discussed the sweet life: exotic journeys to the world's most beautiful hotels, dining at the best and most fashionable restaurants, culture and art. All the finer things in life—the life everyone dreams of. Then the conversation turned to her book about the Danish people. The other guests around the table were surprised by the title, *Happy as a Dane*. "But why did you choose that topic? I can't think of any reason why people in that country would be so happy!" one man said.

The young woman tried to explain the great trust Danes have in one another and in Danish institutions. Their eagerness to contribute to the common good for the benefit of the whole community. The educational system that fosters the development of each student's individual personality. How important it is that all citizens are given the freedom to choose their own way of life and to carve out a place for themselves. Being the best is not what matters so much as finding the right place for oneself. She told them that in her country, they don't try to cultivate a superior elite; their priority is having a population that is happy as a whole. Then she made the mistake of adding that in order to finance that kind of society, the tax burden was the highest in the world, with a marginal tax rate of almost 60 percent for incomes of 390,000 kroner (around $59,000 at the time of this writing, as are all U.S. dollar equivalent amounts given in this book) and above.

At which point the same man lost his patience. "How awful, what a nightmare!" he exclaimed. "Don't try to convince us that a system like that can make anyone happy. Nobody wants to pay for other people. Anyway, without an elite, a country has no future," he continued.

"I watch *Borgen* on TV,"[1] a woman added, "and they're all miserable. This is completely silly, it makes no sense at all!"

Stop. Back to reality.

I am fully aware that the Danish model will not appeal to everyone. My motive for writing this book is in no way to persuade people that this model is better than any other; it is simply my wish to share my experiences and my vision of the world.

I was born, without realizing it, in the happiest country in the world. I wasn't aware how lucky I was, and I decided to leave and make my own way in life. Now, after a long time away from Denmark, I want to review in ten simple key points a model of society that appears to have been making people happy for more than forty years, since we started measuring well-being in countries.

Observers all over the world are in agreement: the Danes are among the happiest people on the planet. Ever since 1973, when one of the first European surveys on the subject was conducted, Denmark has consistently topped international happiness rankings: it came in first in the famous *World Happiness Report* in 2012, 2013 and now 2016 (it's the United Nations' "bible" of happiness levels by country, in which, by way of comparison, Italy came in fiftieth in 2016, France thirty-second, the United Kingdom twenty-third and the United States thirteenth, the highest placement for a country with such a large population). Denmark was also first in the 2012 Eurobarometer survey, first in the 2011 Gallup World Poll (another famous gauge of well-being) and first in the 2008 European Social Survey, among others. An impressive record for a small country whose citizens are generally prone to modesty. So what's the explanation? Why does this small population of around 5.6 million people feel so content when it's cold for nine months of the year and it gets dark at 3 p.m. in winter? When the tax burden is one of the highest in the world, with an income tax of nearly 60 percent, a 170 percent tax on cars and VAT at 25 percent?[2] When the country actually has more pigs (24 million) than people? Quite strange, most people would say!

When the Danes are asked about their status as the happiest nation, they often reply, "Oh yes, I heard about that. I don't know if it's true, but life is definitely good here." They tend not to brag, and certainly not about being the happiest people in the world. Modesty and humility are fundamental cultural values in Denmark. And besides, life isn't a bed of roses there: alcohol and antidepressant consumption remains high, for example, as does the suicide rate (though not nearly as high as rumor has it!). Does that mean Danish happiness isn't real? Not at all. For reasons we're going to discover together, the vast majority of

Danes genuinely feel good about their lives. But in Denmark, like anywhere else, life is complex and you can't make simple generalizations.

I was born in Aarhus, the second largest city in Denmark with 250,000 inhabitants. After growing up in the happiest country in the world, and armed with the knowledge and experience I'd acquired there, I decided to leave—to live my life and find my own personal happiness. At the tender age of eighteen, I wanted to figure out for myself the difference between what people had taught me and what I believed to be the truth about life. Rubbing shoulders with reality is often a good way of putting your points of reference and your beliefs into perspective.

I didn't know back then that the Danish model was an international benchmark of happiness. I'd taken the system for granted; for me, it was normal. That didn't stop me from asking myself hundreds of questions about its major tenets. Is it really a good thing that everyone is equal? Doesn't homogeneity lead to mediocrity? Doesn't the constant emphasis on humility and modesty limit people's potential? And finally, isn't the welfare state just a pretext for taking personal responsibility away from citizens? I also pondered the notion of happiness and where to find it. I needed to put my ideas to the test in real life, to give myself the best chance of becoming independent and free—free to be true to myself.

The path has been a long one. My contact with other countries and cultures has made me more aware of my Danish sense of well-being and to strengthen it. Traveling around Asia, the United States and Europe has opened my eyes to the treasures around me. The country I lost my heart to and where I now live—France—has inspired me through the richness of its culture and people to find my own personal balance and base of well being. So here I am today in France, writing about happiness in Denmark, with all the benefits of hindsight.

Before we explore the secrets of Danish happiness, let's agree on what happiness actually means. Summing it up isn't easy. There is an ocean of definitions and synonyms out there, depending on your language and culture: "joy," "pleasure," "well-being," "bliss," "contentment"—the list goes on. But how best to describe happiness?

There's the very practical scientific point of view: for medical imaging experts, happiness is a specific, measurable state of activity in different parts of the brain. There's also what we learn from etymology: the word "happiness" comes from the Middle English noun "hap," meaning chance or fortune. There are also the very rich observations made by philosophers—from the optimists (Montaigne and Spinoza) to those who believe happiness is impossible (Schopenhauer and Freud). Then there are those who link it to pleasure (Epicurus), to faith (Pascal) and to power (Nietzsche).

And then, most importantly, there's the basic definition, nicely expressed by economist Richard Layard: happiness is "feeling good—enjoying life and wanting the feeling to be maintained."[3] I like this definition because it is simple and resonates with most people.

And let's not forget an important distinction: the difference between the collective happiness of a country (measured by the well-known surveys on happiness) and personal happiness.

There are many factors that influence personal happiness, and I am not sure whether it's possible to measure them in a truly objective way. Even if it is often quite easy to tell the difference between happy and unhappy people, it remains a very intimate, subjective matter. The experts—psychiatrists, sociologists, neuroscientists and education professionals—agree that we are not necessarily equal when it comes to happiness. We can be born with a greater or lesser potential to be happy. Some even argue that genetics are 100 percent responsible for our base level of happiness and that it is therefore predetermined. According to them, each individual's genetic makeup systematically governs their level of happiness. This is called set-point theory, supported by a study in 1996 that examined three hundred sets of twins who had been brought up both together and separately. The research suggested that 80 percent of emotional well-being is determined by genetics.[4] Fortunately, other studies find the ratio to be a more moderate 50 percent. Psychotherapist Thierry Janssen,[5] for example, says that our capacity for happiness is influenced 50 percent by our chromosomes and 10 percent by external factors. The remaining 40 percent is up to us, which still leaves us with plenty of room to maneuver when it comes to our own happiness!

With regard to collective happiness, measured by international surveys, the criteria are different and should be considered with caution. There have been many attempts to define it. For example, the king of Bhutan, a small country in the Himalayas, created a "gross national happiness" (GNH) index in 1972, a wry nod to the classic GDP index, which is based on four criteria: sustainable and equitable socioeconomic development, environmental conservation, the preservation and promotion of culture and good governance.[6] The concept has earned Bhutan the nickname "the happy country," although it has been adversely affected by the economic crisis, and it only comes in eighty-fourth on the World Happiness Report 2016. Another example is the celebrated Club of Rome, founded in 1968 by an alliance of international members with a "common concern for the future of humanity and the planet." The club evaluated happiness, most notably in a 1972 report called *The Limits to Growth*,[7] which argued for the measurement of quality of life by economic indicators.

Whatever the approach, it is inevitable that these global studies have a certain degree of inaccuracy. First, collective happiness cannot be the mathematical sum of individual happiness. Second, many parameters can influence a person's response to a survey question such as "Are you generally satisfied with your life?" It's not an easy question to answer on the spot, as the reply may be influenced by factors as simple as the weather, a major national sporting victory or any positive or negative event that is beyond our control. We might also assume that people who are very unhappy will not bother or feel like taking part in this kind of survey. The organizations that conduct these major surveys, such as the United Nations, Gallup and Eurostat, have also found that even the order of the questions can influence the answers. For example, if the preceding questions relate to politics and corruption levels, the respondents tend to be more negative in their responses about their own satisfaction with life. International rankings can also be criticized for not taking cultural differences into account: the values do not represent the same realities from country to country. Despite these nuances, while this type of major survey may not offer a completely exact picture of a country's collective happiness, the large number of people interviewed means that, at the very least, it provides a reasonably good indication of the average level of happiness or, let's say, well-being of a country's population.

To broaden my ideas on the subject I contacted Christian Bjørnskov, a Danish professor who teaches at Aarhus University and has dedicated his time and energy to the topic for many years. He is also a founding member of the Happiness Research Institute.[8] (Yes, this institute really exists.) In Denmark we have a think tank of generous people who devote themselves exclusively to researching this delightful subject. We spent a whole morning together at Café Casablanca in Aarhus discussing the phenomenon. According to Professor Bjørnskov, there are a number of basic universal factors that contribute to a nation's happiness: a democratic political system, a certain level of national prosperity, a functioning judicial system and the absence of war. He estimates that thirty to forty countries meet these criteria. Once this foundation is in place, other factors influence the level of happiness, in particular trust in others and the freedom (and possibility) to choose one's own way in life.

Whatever the variants and subtle influences, happiness is a universal right. It is even written in black and white in the U.S. Declaration of Independence, drawn up in Boston on July 4, 1776: "We hold these truths to be self-evident, that all men are created equal, that they are endowed by their Creator with certain unalienable Rights, that among these are Life, Liberty and the pursuit of Happiness."

This is why I felt it important to share some of the simple but accessible elements of what constitutes Danish happiness. I have decided to take a very simple approach, while bearing in mind the complexities and scope of the subject, and drawing inspiration from the people I have met and the things I myself have seen and experienced.

Once upon a time, there were ten simple ways to be "happy as a Dane."

1

TRUST

I Have Trust in People

Denmark has the highest level of trust in the world.

t is a glorious summer's day in Denmark. People are outside, making the most of two rare and precious things around here: sunshine and warm weather. I drive into the countryside with my mother to buy fruit and vegetables for dinner. Along the roadside there are stands with potatoes, peas, carrots, raspberries and strawberries for sale. Everything has been grown on the surrounding farms. Nothing very unusual about that. Except for one surprising detail. In Denmark, nobody supervises these stands. Each table has a little pot where you leave money for the produce you've bought. The growers are even considerate enough to leave a few coins, so customers can make change if they need it. The farmer collects his earnings at the end of the day. That's how it was during my childhood and the principle is still respected today. It may be hard to believe, but no one even thinks about stealing. But how in the world does this system work?

AS THE TEMPERATURE DROPS, TRUST RISES

In 2012, Danish professor Gert Tinggaard Svendsen published a book about trust.[1] In it, he compared eighty-six countries to find out where trust does and does not exist.[2] His verdict? Seventy-eight percent of Danes trust those around them. It's a world record—the average rate of trust in the other countries being studied was 25 percent or less. There's no doubt about it: Denmark boasts the highest level of trust in the world. Interestingly, all the Scandinavian countries rank at the top of this survey. Brazil holds one of the lowest positions, with a trust rate of 5 percent. The rest of South America and the African countries join Brazil at the bottom of the list. France and Portugal are below average; more than seven out of ten French people distrust their peers. Americans seem to trust one another at the higher than average rate of 36 percent, whereas the English rank near the average in Europe, at 25 percent.

The study shows that Danes' trust reaches 84 percent when it comes to confidence in institutions (the government, the police, the law and the civil service). Is Professor Svendsen writing this because he's Danish? Hardly. Other researchers, such as Frenchmen Yann Algan and Pierre Cahuc, have also established that the Danes rarely question their institutions.[3] Only 9 percent declare they distrust the police's impartiality—for instance, compared with 15 percent of British and German people, 25 percent of the French and 65 percent of Russians.[4] Moreover, Denmark has been ranked number one in the Forbes World's 10 Best Governments list,[5] which takes into account government powers, absence of corruption, order and security, civil rights, government transparency, regulatory enforcement as well as civil and criminal justice. In 2015 (latest available survey), Denmark had the fairest rule of law of the world (Germany is eighth, the United Kingdom twelfth, France eighteenth, the United States nineteenth and Italy thirtieth).[6]

These findings are loaded with consequences for society. For example: Are you going to pay your income tax willingly if you suspect everyone around you of cheating? Probably not. You'd feel more like a fool than a good citizen. People are more likely to obey rules when they think others are doing the same. In reality, a sustainable welfare state is only possible when it's built on trust among individuals.

Trust not only has a radical impact on how society functions, it also affects personal well-being. Numerous researchers, sociologists, economists and philosophers around the world have tried to define the reasons for happiness. They nearly all agree on one point: trust between individuals is an absolutely crucial factor in the equation. The final word on the subject, the UN's famous *World Happiness Report*,[7] is unequivocal: the more people trust one another, the happier they feel. French researchers Cahuc and Algan also confirm that, conversely, a society built on distrust goes hand in hand with a lower aptitude for happiness.[8] Professor Christian Bjørnskov comes to the same conclusion: "The high level of trust in [Denmark] is one of the most significant explanations for the high level of happiness."[9]

IRRESPONSIBILITY OR TRUST? COATS, WALLETS AND BABIES

At the Copenhagen Opera House, foreigners are always surprised to see Danes leave their coats in an unattended checkroom. It is an example of several hundred people trusting one another instinctively. They know they'll find their personal belongings still there after the performance—it doesn't even cross their minds to think otherwise.

It never crossed mine when I lived in Denmark. One day, my brother returned from the supermarket and told me he had found 500 kroner ($76) in a crate of apples. "Someone must have lost it," he said. He had informed one of the supermarket managers and handed in the money. The rightful owner came back to get her 500 kroner at the end of the day and the manager returned the money to her. As a thank-you she left 100 kroner ($15) for my brother.

This story might seem completely ridiculous to a non-Dane. "How naïve! The manager obviously kept the money for himself," you may say. I can understand a reaction like that. I've lived outside Denmark for more than twenty years. I've seen for myself that distrust is more prevalent than trust—often for good reason, unfortunately. Picture this: you lose your wallet in the street. What hope do you have of getting it back? The answer can be found in an enlightening experiment carried out by *Reader's Digest*.[10] The test organizers dropped eleven hundred wallets in city streets all over the world. Each contained the equivalent of $50 in the local currency along with the wallet owner's contact details. The aim was to see how many people kept them and how many returned them. In the Danish city of Aalborg (130,000 inhabitants), 100 percent of the wallets were returned with the money. The average across all cities was slightly over 50 percent. The experiment showed that the chance of recovering your belongings in many countries, including Mexico, China, Italy and Russia, is very low. In the United States as well as in the United Kingdom, 67 percent of people returned the wallet, which is quite a good score.

Trust is one of those things that can change everything in life, because it brings peace of mind. One day, my mother had €300 ($337) in cash stolen in Paris. Her Danish insurance company asked if she could prove she had withdrawn that sum that day. Unfortunately she hadn't kept the ATM receipt, the only immediately available evidence. But even without proof, the company trusted her and reimbursed the entire amount. A few years later, when I had the same bad luck in Paris, the person I spoke to at my French insurance company just kept repeating the same thing: "You're joking, aren't you?"

Another example: I worked in a café in Copenhagen for three years to finance my studies. The place was known for all the strollers that new mothers on maternity leave would park outside while they chatted with their friends inside. Non-Danes often find it surprising, but in Denmark it's normal for babies to be left outside restaurants and cafés while the parents are inside. In one respect, no one is keeping an eye on them, but in another, everyone is—because, to reiterate, people have trust in those around them.

This custom caused a scandal in New York a few years ago. A young Danish woman had left her baby in a stroller outside a restaurant while she and the child's father ate together inside. The restaurant called the police and the mother was arrested for abandoning her child. The U.S. authorities kept the baby for three or four days before giving her back to her mother.

BACKSTABBING-FREE ZONE

In August 2012, Danish financial newspaper *Børsen* organized a large conference on the theme of trust.[11] Stephen M. R. Covey, an expert on the subject and best-selling author of *The Speed of Trust*, was naturally invited to speak.[12] He began by paying tribute to Denmark as *the* model of trust. Then he focused on the extremely high costs associated with a lack of trust. In an organization where individuals have misgivings about one another, very expensive monitoring, compliance and security mechanisms must be put in place. Covey cited well-known American investor Warren Buffett and one of his major acquisitions— McLane Company, the distribution business of Walmart Stores, whose revenues totaled $23 billion. Typically, a merger of this size would take months and cost a fortune in lawyers', consultants' and auditors' fees as both sides have to be scrutinized inside out. But in this case, the two parties liked and trusted each other. The deal was made in two hours and sealed with a handshake, saving months of work and millions of dollars. In Covey's opinion, "distrust doubles the cost of doing business."[13]

The then Danish economy minister, Margrethe Vestager, also attended the conference. For nearly an hour (and without notes), she also maintained that trust was a source of economic savings, explaining, for instance, that it costs far less to trust the unemployed than to keep them under surveillance. She clings to this conviction to this day now that she is in charge of the Competition portfolio in the European Commission. It should be noted that the Danes are very proud of their welfare system. A survey done in 2009 for Danish daily newspaper *Jyllands-Posten* confirmed that it was what they are most satisfied with,[14] more

so even than the democracy, tolerance and peace in their country. But they know it's vital that every citizen participates and
contributes, without acting fraudulently or cheating. Honesty
in job seekers is perceived as being not only in their own interest but in the common interest too. Vestager admitted that a
minimum of supervision is nevertheless necessary, even in
Denmark. In September 2012, a controversy broke out. A young
man nicknamed "Lazy Robert" by the press scandalized the
entire country. Lazy Robert publicly declared that he preferred
taking advantage of unemployment benefits rather than accept
what he considered to be a boring job with a fast-food chain.
How could someone deliberately cash in on the system without
being ashamed? It is quite clear that Lazy Robert is not the only
one with this kind of attitude, but this was really shocking to
the Danes. The idea seems to bother people less in France perhaps. One day, a young French woman told me about her excit-
ing adventures living in America. "Sounds fantastic, but how
did you earn a living without a green card?" I asked her. "I'm on
unemployment!" she replied, not in the least embarrassed. In
another instance, someone I once sat next to at dinner proudly
told me he had taken a year's sabbatical courtesy of unemployment benefits. He just wanted to hang out for a while, thinking
about life and enjoying some free time!

In any event, I left the *Børsen* conference with a big smile on
my face. I was happy for my country. And I reminded myself to
remember to pay the €750 ($840) attendance fee. That's right—
the organizers hadn't asked for advance payment; they trusted
participants to pay later. As former Danish prime minister Poul
Nyrup Rasmussen once said, "You rarely see a Dane with a knife
in one hand, without a fork in the other."[15]

SWINDLES AND CROOKED DEALS

When I had my first job in Paris, I called my father to tell him about an extremely kind offer a printer had made to me. "He's giving us a great deal on our brochures—he's going to print them for less than the other printers, plus he owns a lovely apartment in my dream neighborhood and is willing to rent it to me for a very reasonable price. Isn't that kind?" "Yes," my father replied, "but what will you do the day he raises his prices? If you live in an apartment he owns and you pay below-market rent, you'll find yourself in a rather tricky situation, don't you think?"

Obviously the answer was "yes," and I didn't accept the offer. I even chose another printer. My first reaction was based on the idea that as he was offering better value for money than the others, it was fine to give him the contract, especially as he was also being kind by giving me a deal on the apartment. It seemed like a win-win situation. In actual fact, it would have been fraught with problems. By accepting his offer, I would have lost my independence and impartiality in our business partnership. I would have been personally motivated to keep the contract with that particular supplier on behalf of a company where I was just an employee.

When I tell people this anecdote I get a variety of reactions. Some say (mostly southern Europeans, admittedly), "How silly of you! Imagine how lovely it would have been to live in that apartment!" While other friends (often Danish) are infuriated: "How awful! He was trying to bribe you. What a shady offer— good thing you didn't accept it." The dictionary definition of corruption is "the abuse of power for personal gain." In its own modest way, this is a perfect example.

Corruption in Denmark is actually the lowest in the world, alongside Finland and New Zealand. Transparency International, a corruption-fighting organization, published its most recent annual corruption survey in July 2013.[16] Of the 107 countries featured, Denmark comes out on top of the world's lowest bribery rate (and it was already the case in the previous report) along with Finland, Japan and Australia. Among developed countries, Spain is in second place, the United Kingdom and Italy are fifth, Switzerland and the United States are seventh, while Greece is only nineteenth. Emerging countries such as Mexico (twenty-seventh), Indonesia (twenty-ninth), South Africa (thirty-sixth) and India (thirty-ninth) are far after the average rate and still struggle with high levels of corruption. Afghanistan, Kenya and Sierra Leone appear at the very bottom of the list. Interestingly, Transparency International also provides another index, focused on perceived corruption by citizens. There have been three reports to date (in 2013, 2014 and 2015), each time ranking Denmark (alone) as the country where the perception of corruption was the lowest.[17]

Generally speaking, corruption in Denmark's government institutions and business sector is very low. The Danes simply don't tolerate it. Over 90 percent say that "accepting bribery in the workplace is unjustifiable." The percentage of people who agree with this statement stands at just over 50 percent in France, 75 percent in Portugal and 80 percent in America.[18]

Punishing corruption plays a crucial role in setting an example. One of Denmark's most famous corruption cases broke in 2002. Peter Brixtofte, then-mayor of the city of Farum and a popular politician, was accused of abusing the system and the public good. The scandal started with a press revelation about a $22,500 restaurant bill (including wildly expensive bottles of wine) that Brixtofte had claimed as expenses for "various council meetings." Other examples of fraud surfaced, including incidents that benefited his friends. The case deeply shocked the Danes and Brixtofte was soon expelled from political life. After several appeals, he was finally sentenced to two years' imprisonment.

In 2004, the Danish International Development Agency (Danida)—part of the Ministry of Foreign Affairs—launched an Action Plan to Fight Corruption and developed a Code of Conduct, establishing a zero-tolerance policy. They apply to Danida's own development aid staff, as well as to stakeholders, partners and aid beneficiaries. An Anti-Corruption Hotline has even been set up, enabling people to report instances of corruption anonymously.

When a nation's relationship with their politicians, institutions and financial bodies is based on trust, they have a better foundation for living a happy life. In my opinion, this is one of the main reasons behind the Danes' widespread happiness.

EDUCATION

I Have a Place in Society

Education in Denmark is tailored to develop the
personality and skills of every student; it does
not seek to create an elite. Education is free and
students even receive State grants,
so it is accessible to all.[1]

t was my first day at London South Bank University for a term
abroad as part of my course at Niels Brock Copenhagen Business
College. I was sitting in the main lecture hall with three hundred other students, all of us listening attentively to the professor.
At the end of his introduction, he looked around the auditorium
and said, "One last point for our Danish students: we aren't interested in your personal opinions here. You must back up what you
say by quoting recognised authorities."

I was a bit surprised by the warning, wondering if the professor had something against Danes! But it wasn't that at all,
simply that one of the well-known goals of the Danish education system is to create independent individuals by developing
their curiosity and opinions rather than by emphasizing subject
knowledge learned by heart. Children in Denmark are encouraged to experience things for themselves and to form their

own points of view. The system endeavors to educate tomorrow's citizens so they understand their rights, responsibilities and duties in a society built on equality, solidarity and liberty. Danish schools also put a great deal of energy into developing self-esteem in students, and encourage them to form their own personalities so they can face the future under the best circumstances.

I THINK FOR MYSELF, THEREFORE I AM

Are the Danes completely crazy? Not completely. The benefits of independence and participation on learning is an accepted concept in cognitive science and education theory. At the Organisation for Economic Co-operation and Development (OECD), the advanced researchers at the Centre for Educational Research and Innovation (CERI) are unanimous: the human brain learns better when people experiment, participate and make their own suggestions, rather than when they receive knowledge passively from the top down.[2] This is nothing new. Socrates long ago understood that the mind works best when it "gives birth" to understanding and has to find solutions itself. It's what the OECD and UNESCO have coined "21st-Century Skills," which include collaboration and communication, critical thinking and problem solving, creativity and innovation, and initiative and self-direction.[3] These are the qualities most sought after by today's employers and the most useful for our connected society.

Developing the personality is also the focus of two types of school in Denmark that have no real equivalent abroad: the *efterskole* and the *højskole*. Danish schoolchildren between the ages of fourteen and eighteen can choose to spend one to three years in a residential *efterskole* (literally "after school"). The aim is to develop students' potential in areas other than traditional school subjects in order to help them find a place for themselves in society, even if they don't excel in a traditional academic environment. The emphasis is on creativity, sport, vocational skills and group activities, delivered in an atmosphere of solidarity and freedom. After attending an *efterskole*, many students find their proper place in life, having acquired the confidence they need to achieve personal fulfillment. There are around 260 *efterskoler* in Denmark. Efterskoleforeningen, the association of *efterskole*, confirms that it is a very popular schooling option among young Danes, with over 15 percent of students enrolled in an *efterskole* each year.

A report by Damvad Analytics for Efterskoleforeningen published in September 2012 covering the period 2000–2010 concludes that students who have attended an *efterskole* are more likely not only to start but to finish an upper secondary or vocational training (*ungdomsuddannelse*) and, as a result, find the right role for themselves in society. The authors observed that, thanks to the prevailing spirit of solidarity in these schools, the students from tough social backgrounds are inspired and helped by more advantaged children. Endless positive accounts back this up, including one Emma Rytter Hansen shared with me during a lengthy discussion we had.[4] Emma was enrolled in an *efterskole* for a year before taking her end of high school exams. She explained that the experience had taught her how to accept and respect the differences of others through dialogue and tolerance. "I was a real rebel at school and behaved badly all the time. I dreamed of getting a second chance." Emma was taught to get to know herself and others so she could function better in a system in which the well-being of the group comes before one's personal goals. "I realized the huge value of living in a community where there is a place for everyone, a world in which no one is excluded and where problems are resolved through dialogue."

These schools nevertheless have strict rules. Any illegal act, such as drug use, theft and violence, can lead to expulsion. Emma recalled a young girl who had caused trouble at her school by repeatedly lying and stealing money. "We spent a lot of time talking to her as a group, but after six months, the administration decided she was jeopardizing the group's well-being and harmony. They expelled her and she was transferred to social services, who take over particularly difficult cases. 'Solidarity,' 'tolerance' and 'confidence' are the keywords, but the system has to be respected by everyone."

Emma wrapped up our conversation by saying: "That year changed me. It created a solid foundation on which to build a future that is in line with the person I am." Good for her, I say, and for Danish society, which helped foster another happy Dane!

The other unique Danish school is the *højskole*. Imagine a school whose principal goal is to instill in students the desire to learn. A place where everyone can express themselves freely and ask any kind of question, led by curiosity or simply in search of answers. That school exists in Denmark. It was founded in the nineteenth century by Lutheran bishop N. F. S. Grundtvig, who was also a linguist, historian and educator, and who is considered to be the father of the concept of "lifelong learning." Grundtvig believed in an education based on the notion of pleasure, one that embodied fundamental values such as equality, respecting others, sharing and contributing to the group. He conceived a school that was accessible to all, a sort of school of life, where students could express their creativity and learn to live as part of a community. He conceived it to be a free education, without competition or diplomas.

Grundtvig's first *højskole* was founded in 1844, in Roeddinge. Today, there are over sixty-nine *højskoles* located throughout Denmark. The average age of the students is estimated to be twenty-four, but people of all ages attend. They share a desire for an enriching personal experience. In keeping with the original philosophy, getting into a *højskole* is quite easy. You have to be a minimum of seventeen years old and speak one of the school's working languages, Danish or English. Course lengths vary from one week to ten months. The system is partially subsidized by the State through student grants and funding paid directly to the schools. According to the Institution of Danish Statistics, in 2012 nearly ten thousand Danes took a long course in a *højskole* and forty-five thousand took a short course. An estimated one in ten Danes takes a course in a *højskole* in their lifetime.[5]

SCHOOL: A BED OF ROSES?

In 2012, Danish television channel DR1 ran a documentary series following a class in Denmark and a class in China in their final year of compulsory education.[6] The aim was to compare the Danish schoolchildren's abilities with those of the Chinese, who are among the best-performing students in the world.[7]

The Chinese schoolchildren came out ahead by a long shot in nearly every subject, outshining the Danes even in self-discipline.

The program provoked a huge debate in the media. Was the Danish school model still valid in light of international competition? Did the system, and even the very foundations of Danish education, need to be radically reviewed? Possibly. But the comparison was concerned only with academic results and didn't take the students' well-being into account. Nor did it consider their ability to develop their personal skills so that they might choose a career that suited their personalities. When you read that a third of students in OECD countries find no pleasure in studying,[8] and that almost three-quarters of young people in France say they are bored in secondary school,[9] it gives you plenty of food for thought. In another study the OECD did on an international scale, the results showed that U.S. students reached only an international average of engagement at school, and were worse off than Germany, Japan, Korea and China.[10]

The Danish education system doesn't cultivate an elite or place importance on being the best. Elites around the world only represent very few people, after all. There's no official cut-off for what makes one "an elite," but I think it's safe to assume between about 1 percent and 5 percent of a country's population. For reasons of common sense or simply because of their life philosophy, the Danes tend to be more interested in the remaining 95–99 percent of the population. What guides education in Denmark is teaching knowledge so the majority of students can follow. The level is adjusted to suit the majority, not the high achievers, to make sure no one is left out. The key goal of the Danish education system is not for students to shine through the knowledge they have acquired, but for each individual to feel valued for his or her own particular skills and personality. For all students to realize they have a place and use in society.

In 1999, toward the end of my business studies at Niels Brock in Copenhagen, I met with four people from my class to prepare for a group examination—another uniquely Danish phenomenon. The concept was introduced in 1993 by the then-socialist government, with the aim of cultivating group cohesion and team spirit.[11] It involves group work in the form of a written project followed by an oral exam. During the latter, each member of the group presents and is individually graded, but the grades are strongly influenced by the group's collective performance. In 2006, Denmark's right-wing government abandoned the initiative, claiming it didn't properly evaluate students' individual merits.[12] The decision caused anger among students. True to their Danish spirit, they appreciated having that kind of solidarity around a collaborative project. The group exam ended up being reinstated in 2012, with schools being left to decide whether to implement it or not.[13] Which is in itself a very Danish solution too!

Higher education in Denmark is also free and even subsidized by the government through grants paid to every student of 5,900 kroner ($890) per month regardless of financial need. By way of comparison, around 30 percent of students in France are awarded a grant of up to €545 ($615) per month for ten months of the year based on their parents' income.[14] In Germany it goes up to €670 ($756) per month (but half of the amount is a scholarship, the other half is a zero-rate loan).[15] Finland, Sweden, Norway, Ireland and the Czech Republic also provide free higher education. In many other countries, however, students have to pay to go to a university. Tuition fees are generally between €400 and €1,200 ($450 and $1,350, respectively) per year in France (but skyrocket into the tens of thousands of

Euros at the prestigious and competitive French *grandes écoles*—
compare that to Copenhagen Business School, Scandinavia's
foremost establishment, where tuition is completely free), as
well as in Spain, Italy, Austria, Switzerland, Belgium and Portugal. Annual student fees rise to the equivalent of around €3,000
($3,300) in New Zealand; €4,000 ($4,500) in Australia, Canada
and Japan; €5,000 ($5,600) in Korea.[16] Student fees have tripled
between 2009 and 2012 in the United Kingdom (except Scot-
land), going from £3,000 to £9,000 ($4,300 to $12,910, respec-
tively)![17] In the United States, there are many variations among
institutions but we can say that state universities cost an average of $9,139; in private universities you'll have to pay an aver-
age of $31,231.[18]

In developed countries, young people often wonder what
courses of study or jobs to pursue in order to earn a high salary.
For example, 19.1 percent of young people in the United Kingdom and 31.15 percent in the United States think it's important
to have a higher level of material comfort than their parents,
compared with only 11.8 percent of young Danes. The proportion
of young people whose ambition is to earn a lot of money over
the next fifteen years is 33 percent in Italy, 30 percent in France
and 29 percent in the United States, compared with 18 percent
in Denmark. Young Danish people say that it is more important
for them to pass down the values of tolerance, respect, responsibility, honesty and independence to their children than it is
an inheritance.[19]

When you are guided by the thought of material success, you
run the risk of taking the wrong path, because you turn your
back on your true desires in favor of financial gain. Many people find themselves in careers that don't have any real mean-

ing for them, but in Denmark, schools focus on giving students the best advice to enable them to choose the higher studies or training courses that will lead to the most meaningful life for them. Higher education and career advice is very much tailored to the individual. It has even been given the status of a public service, with municipality-run centers set up to help young people make realistic decisions about their future opportunities. As well as organizing group advice and exchange sessions, these centers examine each student's plan individually.[20] Interestingly, 60 percent of young Danes believe they can choose how their life will pan out, compared with 26 percent in France and 23 percent in Germany. Almost half of young Danes think they have complete freedom and control over their future.[21]

Danish schools are also more likely to teach subjects less commonly taught in other countries, such as sex education. During these classes, Danish students learn about sexual intercourse, how to protect themselves and how to express their boundaries and their desires. Sex isn't a taboo subject in Denmark. On the contrary, it is considered one of life's pleasures. In the 1970s and 1980s, the Scandinavians had quite a reputation abroad for being sexually free, which certainly shocked citizens of more religiously oriented nations. Where I come from, we think that having a well-balanced life includes having a fulfilling sex life. And Danish schoolchildren are encouraged to discuss sex openly and ask questions freely.

By putting the emphasis on students' individual development, skills and abilities instead of on celebrating high achievement, the Danish system facilitates the pursuit of personal happiness. Yet again, enjoyment of school and a good education go hand in hand. According to the latest Program for International

Student Assessment (PISA) survey, which compares the key knowledge and skills levels of fifteen-year-olds in the sixty-five OECD member and partner countries, students who enjoy studying perform 20 percent better at school than those who don't.[22]

But does this mean it's a bed of roses? No, of course not. Even if the general level of education remains satisfactory,[23] the inevitable major risk of this system is that it doesn't adequately develop the potential of very gifted students, so their skills diminish over time. I went to visit my old school, Skaade Skole, in Aarhus to find out more. I discussed the issue with the assistant principal, Jesper Kousholt, a young man who is absolutely passionate about his job and about his students' development. He estimates that around 5 percent of students are understimulated in the Danish system and admits that the smartest are often neglected because it is believed they don't need the support. Yet Kousholt holds the Danish education system in very high regard. He thinks it's important to focus on 95 percent of the students rather than on the gifted few, but he nevertheless believes the system should come up with a better way of developing the potential of the remaining 5 percent.[24]

I see this wish to empower top students as a potential area of progress for Denmark, and a real opportunity, but it won't be an easy balance to strike.

JUMPING IN, BUT NOT DROWNING

Tal Ben-Shahar is a preeminent happiness guru who taught positive psychology at Harvard, where his classes were among the most popular in the university's history. During his teach-

ing career he observed that students generally dislike schoolwork. He puts forward two models to explain what motivates
them to study: the "drowning" model and the "lovemaking"
model. [25] "Drowning" is a system of suffering and then being
freed from pain and feeling relief, which students may mistake
for a kind of happiness. If your head is held under water, you
will fight to come up for air. Once above water, you will feel
relieved and even (fleetingly) happy. Ben-Shahar explains that
the pain/relief cycle is the overriding pattern experienced by
schoolchildren from as early as the primary level. This illustrates why the majority of young people associate schoolwork
with anguish and short-lived interludes of respite (for example,
weekends). Recent surveys in France confirm that nearly three-
quarters of students don't like going to school very much or at
all, that 65 percent of them have a recurring fear of failure and
that almost 70 percent sometimes don't understand what they
are being asked to do in their lessons. [26] Another recent survey
unveils that high school students in the United States associate
school with negative words (eight of the top ten responses were
derogatory), principally "tired" (for 39 percent of the respondents), "stressed" (29 percent) and "bored" (26 percent). [27] Indeed,
American students experience the highest level of stress in a
survey comparing nine advanced economies, far before Canada
(second), the United Kingdom (third), France and Germany
(both fourth). [28]

Ben-Shahar's second model, "lovemaking," is when students
are motivated because they find learning enjoyable. Reading,
researching, thinking, asking questions and finding answers
are activities that can bring satisfaction and even pleasure, if
taught in the right way. Students need to learn to find happiness

in the actual process of learning and not to think of studying as a form of suffering they are desperate to escape.

Parents can also put pressure on their children by expecting them to be the best and to have good marks. Academic success may be much more important to them than their child's enjoyment of learning. They may be reluctant to let their children pursue other options should their studies not suit their profile, abilities or wishes.

Ben-Shahar adds that to contribute to our children's happiness, we should guide them toward a path that brings them meaning and pleasure. Whatever their ambitions and passions, it's crucial we help make them aware of the pros and cons of their choices. After students have weighed their options, parents and teachers should encourage them on their chosen path. This pretty much sums up the approach of the Danish education system, so it must have something to do with our famous happiness.

The students I met at Skaade Skole in August, just before the start of the new school year, support this statement. They were about to embark on their final year of compulsory education (ninth *klasse*) before going on to upper secondary school or opting for vocational training. The general consensus was that they were free to choose their future without pressure from either their parents or society. One girl commented, "What's good in Denmark is that you aren't afraid to pursue what you like doing, because if you happen to make a mistake, the State's there to help you get back onto your feet." Several of the students were drawn to the option of spending a year at *efterskole* to get to know themselves better and to explore more imaginative career choices. When it came to discussing money and whether it influenced their plans, they were unanimous. They would prefer to have a job they liked than to earn a lot of money.

My own personal experience was that I was free to choose what I studied and my parents always supported my choices. When I was nine, I told my parents I wanted to be a Danish ambassador. They explained the career to me carefully, stressing that before I could settle in London or Paris I'd have to spend time in many far-off countries, but not necessarily those I dreamed of visiting. At the age of eleven, having thought long and hard about it, I announced that I would like to work in the hotel industry instead. My father arranged a meeting for me with the director of the nicest hotel in town and told me to prepare my questions beforehand. We went to meet the director together and I put all my queries to her. She explained that working in a hotel was a way of life, not a job in the classic sense. "You have to work evenings and weekends in this profession, so you have to be passionate about it in order to be happy."

I looked into the possibility of going to hotel school abroad, but it was so expensive that I dropped the idea and looked for another path that would suit me. Finding your vocation isn't easy; it requires a lot of time and willpower to achieve your goal. And if education systems are simply geared toward churning out high-achieving students, it only makes the task more difficult.

With the support and confidence of my parents, I was able to take exactly the direction I wanted to in life. Above all, they wanted me to be happy. My mother and father always encouraged me to go find my own happiness. They supported me in all my decisions, in spite of the anxiety they must have sometimes caused them.

FREEDOM AND INDEPENDENCE

I Am Free to Choose My Own Way in Life

Nearly 70 percent of young Danes leave home
at the age of eighteen to lead independent lives,
which to a large extent prevents social pressure
from parents.

I was just nine years old when I got my first job. My grand-mother had told me about a modeling agency that was look-ing for girls to photograph. I asked my parents' permission and my mother took me to meet the head of the agency, who offered to sign me to the agency. I was thrilled at the prospect of earning my own pocket money. My modeling career didn't last long. By the age of thirteen (the minimum legal age for working without your parents' permission), I decided to find another job. I was hired by a little shop in Aarhus Hospital to take a small cart filled with newspapers around the wards and sell them to patients. I used to roll it up and down the corridors, shout-ing "Newspapers and magazines!" It was great fun and I really enjoyed going there twice a week after school—until the day the manager accused me of stealing a magazine from the cart.

I quit, saying we could no longer work together if she didn't trust me. I remember how proud my mother was when I told her about my reaction.

GIVING YOURSELF THE MEANS TO BE INDEPENDENT

Practically all my friends had evening or weekend jobs. In Denmark, almost 70 percent of young people between the ages of thirteen and seventeen have a job outside of school; that figure rises to over 80 percent after the age of seventeen. Even though it's difficult to draw comparisons between one country and the next because statistical methods vary, it can safely be said that it's quite a high proportion. At a much later stage in Ireland, Austria, Finland and Germany, 65–70 percent of students have paid jobs during their university years while fewer than half do in Spain (49 percent), France (47 percent) and Portugal (20 percent).[1] In the United States, 80 percent of students work; tuition fees are so high that many students work to avoid taking out as many loans or for spending money.[2] The jobs female students take in Denmark usually consist of babysitting, cleaning and working as sales assistants in bakeries or newsstands, while male students do newspaper rounds or sort bottles for supermarkets (in Denmark, empty bottles are worth 1 krone each, to encourage people to return them instead of littering).

According to a survey conducted by the Danish Centre for Youth Research,[3] the primary motivation for young people to work is being able to pay for their activities themselves. This gives them greater independence from their parents as they don't have to keep asking them for money, and thus permission, for activities. The survey also confirms that young people from wealthier families are just as likely to work as those who aren't. It has nothing to do with how much their parents earn—young Danes simply want a degree of autonomy.

This spirit of self-sufficiency isn't specific to the young; it's deeply ingrained in the Danish psyche. A good illustration of our celebration of independence is Christiania, an autonomous district in Copenhagen that was founded as a self-proclaimed "free town" in 1971 on the site of a former military barracks. It started out as an experiment for a handful of artists and free-thinkers, but gradually new inhabitants arrived and Christiania became a permanent part of the capital, albeit with its own set of rules and no taxes for residents. According to its mission statement, "The objective of Christiania is to create a self-governing society in which each individual holds themselves responsible for the well-being of the entire community." It's a vibrant place that attracts hordes of visitors, but it is also a source of controversy—for example, cannabis is openly sold there. A conflict arose in 2006 when the right-wing government declared that this type of alternative system was illegal, not to mention unfair, given that every other Dane paid income tax. In 2011 the State finally reached an agreement with Christiania residents, allowing them to buy their land and earn the legal right to stay.[4] It's a perfect example of how highly the Danes value their autonomy.

I didn't go as far as moving to Christiania to acquire my independence. At the age of fifteen, my best friend and I took a job cleaning the offices of an accounting firm two evenings a week. It was very well paid and although the work was not particularly interesting in itself, I used to amuse myself by making up stories about the people who worked in the offices. There were the tidy ones, the messy ones, the ones who scarfed down sweets on their own and the ones who shared them with the office. In no way did I see the job as embarrassing or degrading. It was a job like any other, perfect for earning a bit of pocket money—the key to independence.

When I was eighteen, I started paying rent at home. I was happy to contribute and thought it natural that I should help my mother, who was a single parent after getting divorced from my father. That summer, after taking my final exams, I went to live in Paris. In Denmark it is very common for young people to leave home at the age of eighteen in search of independence. According to a Eurostat report,[5] Denmark holds the world record for the highest number of people who leave home between the ages of eighteen and twenty-four. Only 34 percent of them still live with their parents, compared with 62 percent in France, 70 percent in England and over 80 percent in Spain and Italy. In the United States, 31 percent of eighteen- to thirty-four-year-olds live with their parents.[6] In the twenty-five to thirty-four age group, 98 percent of Danes have flown the nest.

But this raises an important issue: What should be done with this freedom? How should it be handled? Being able to choose your life and have sole responsibility for your destiny is wonderful. But it can also prove daunting. Could this in some way explain the relatively high suicide rate in Scandinavian countries? According to the World Health Organization, 22.2 men out of 100,000 commit suicide in Finland, 18.7 in Sweden and 13.6 in Denmark. The countries with the highest number of male suicides per 100,000 of the population are Guyana (70.8), Lithuania (51.0), Sri Lanka (46.6), Surinam (44.5) and Korea

(41.7). By comparison, the figure stands at 35.1 in Russia, 26.9 in Japan, 19.3 in France and the United States, 14.5 in Germany, 9.8 in the United Kingdom, 8.2 in Spain and 7.6 in Italy. Among the countries with the lowest suicide rates are Libya (2.2), Iraq (1.2), Kuwait (1.0) and Syria (0.7),[7] yet life in those countries can be considered quite difficult and with limited freedom.

A similar phenomenon exists in the United States. Economists studied a sample of 2.3 million Americans, state by state, asking them whether they were satisfied or dissatisfied with their lives. Then they compared the results with the number of suicides in the same state. It emerged that Utah, the happiest state in the United States, is ninth when it comes to suicides. Ditto for Hawaii: number two in happiness rankings, it has the fifth highest number of suicides.[8] Could it be that when people live in a fulfilling, positive environment and are openly encouraged to find the best path in life, they are more likely to say to themselves that they are to blame if things don't work out, not their circumstances? There's no simple answer—it is a very complex phenomenon that's rooted in a whole set of sensitive issues, on both a personal and collective level. Nevertheless, it's important to consider these kinds of questions and not sweep the subject under the rug.

SHAREHOLDERS IN SHORTS

In Denmark, young people's independence is also facilitated by the student grant system. As we saw in the last chapter, the State awards students in higher education 5,900 kroner ($890) a month, regardless of the financial situation of their parents. And there are no tuition fees, so education is accessible to all.[9] This system allows each and every young person to freely choose what to study without being dependent on their parents' income.

I believe this is one of the reasons why Denmark is a country of such high social mobility. When we talk about social mobility, we may instinctively think of people from low-income families. But it gives freedom to young people from well-off families too. Why would it help children who are already at an advantage, you may ask? Because, paradoxically, their parents' income doesn't always guarantee them freedom at all. I have been fortunate enough to travel a lot and I've observed, all over the world, that parents in privileged families tend to impose career choices on their children. Since they are the ones paying for education, they are more likely to pressure their children into careers that make the parents happy, often steering them toward those with high social status, so as to maintain levels of professional achievement and income already attained by previous generations. I have also noticed in these situations that career pressure is often joined by emotional pressure concerning the choice of partner, especially for daughters: parents tend to guide them toward people from their own social backgrounds.

This type of scenario is rarely witnessed in Denmark because social differences aren't as pronounced. The United Nations Development Programme has established that it's one of the most egalitarian countries in the world[10] (which we will come back to in a later chapter). Equality for all is one of the most deeply rooted values in our country, as is modesty (which I will be looking at in the coming pages as well). These factors tend to reduce parental pressure on young Danes over their futures.

A Council of Europe report put it succinctly: "The decision to complete higher education is becoming less and less correlated with parental background in Denmark."[11]

By the age of eleven, I'd earned around €1,300 ($1,460) from my brief modeling career. I informed my parents that I'd thought about it and wanted to open an account with Danske Bank, even though my parents were long-standing customers of a different bank. The reason for my decision was that the manager of Danske Bank frequently came to dinner parties at my parents' house. My brother and I were always invited to sit at the table with their guests, which usually included clients of my father's law firm. I'd observed this man on several occasions and thought he looked very serious—the ideal person to look after my money. So my mother took me to the local branch. I also used some of my money to buy my first shares, because I thought being a shareholder sounded even more exciting.

I admit this is rather extreme behavior and highly unusual for a child, but it nevertheless illustrates the desire young Danes have for independence. It is quite striking how many Danish children have their own bank accounts. Most of the Danish children I know today, and the ones I knew when I was a child, are account holders.

This culture of independence can also give children wings and make them bold. It may explain the rather cavalier action I took to get my first proper job interview. After two gap years in Paris and Copenhagen, I decided it was time to go back to school. One morning, as I was leafing through the Danish financial newspaper *Børsen*, I came across an article written about an extraordinary woman—the beautiful daughter of a Danish ambassador. Thanks to her father's job, she had lived in every exotic country in the world. It went on to describe the various stages of her career path, leading up to an impressive job in the cosmetics industry. She had just been appointed managing director of high-end Danish audio and video company Bang & Olufsen in France. I said to myself, "Wow, I want to be like her. I'm going to ask her how she did it." So I looked up her number and called her assistant, who wasn't convinced by this young Danish woman's request to speak to her boss and refused to put me through. I called every day for a month. One day, I finally wore her down and she let me speak to her. I explained to Elisabeth that my ambition was to pursue the same career path she had, and I begged her to grant me fifteen minutes of her time. She agreed to meet me in her offices in La Plaine Saint-Denis, just north of Paris. During our half-hour meeting, I told her I wanted to work for her, even unpaid if necessary, just to soak up her experience. To test me out, she sent me to the Lyon International Fair for two weeks to run a museum-style stand of vintage Bang & Olufsen equipment. Her thinking was that if I pulled it off, she'd hire me—and that's how I landed my first proper job. After the fair, Elisabeth offered me a work/study contract at Bang & Olufsen in Paris. I enrolled in a marketing and international business course at Niels Brock Business School and lived between Paris and Copenhagen for three years. In Elisabeth, I'd found the perfect professional mentor. What she taught me during the six years I worked with her provided me with foundations that are still crucial to my professional life today.

Behind these anecdotes about pocket money and perseverance lies a deeper message that is very revealing about Danish culture: that setting free and asserting a child's personality from a very young age leads to fulfillment in adult life, even if the path is sometimes rocky. It's the same message found in Hans Christian Andersen's famous story *The Little Mermaid*. She has to challenge her father's authority in order to follow her heart and finally finds happiness on land. Or his tale of the Ugly Duckling, who has to accept that he isn't like the rest of his family in order to become who he really is. This is one of the fundamental underpinnings of Danish happiness: our freedom to become who we want to be.

4

EQUAL OPPORTUNITY

I Can Become Whomever I Want

The country in the world with the highest social
mobility is actually Denmark.

W hat I'm about to say may be rather controversial, but
I'll come out and say it anyway: the so-called American dream is actually Danish. First of all, what exactly
is the American dream? It's the beautiful idea that everyone can
create their own success, no matter their starting point. Put less
romantically, it is what economists and sociologists call social
mobility: the ability of one generation to do better, or at least
differently, than its parents' generation. This social mobility
is inextricably linked to the concepts we have just discussed,
namely, personal freedom and independence.

COPENHAGEN SIDE STORY

So that's the American dream. Except that, according to a study
by the OECD,[1] it is a lot easier to climb the social ladder in Scandinavian countries such as Denmark than in France, Italy, Great
Britain or even, surprisingly, the United States. That's right:
social mobility in the United States is not as fluid as you may

think. According to the "Great Gatsby curve," which portrays the correlation between inequality and intergenerational social mobility,[2] the United States lags far behind France, Japan and, of course, Denmark.

What makes a society more or less mobile? The OECD's findings show that social mobility from one generation to the next is generally greater in societies that are more egalitarian. The Danish social security and tax system is, in fact, highly redistributive—in other words, it seeks to reduce the gap between the lowest and highest income earners. We'll discuss this more fully in the following chapters.

The OECD also places great emphasis on the role of education policies in increasing mobility. A system that favors universal access to education, such as by providing financial support if necessary, substantially increases equal opportunities. In countries where financial support is available for every student—like Denmark, as we have seen—children from less-privileged families have a better chance of going on to higher education.

That said, social mobility remains one of the most important and sensitive political issues for the Danish government. Even though we are among the highest-ranking countries in the world in this respect, socioeconomic background nonetheless continues to be a determining factor when it comes to success or level of education.

I was about eight years old when my parents decided to enroll me in a private school. In 2012 there were some 537 private schools in Denmark and 1,754 state schools, of which 436 were specialized schools. Eighty-seven percent of funding for private schools comes from the government, but parents contribute by paying the equivalent of around €150–€200 ($170–$225) per month.[3]

The students who attended the private school I went to, Foraeldreskolen, mostly came from privileged backgrounds, but in every class, two or three students were there on scholarships, which meant that their parents didn't have to pay the additional tuition. Ultimately, my class had a fairly good socioeconomic mix.

My best friend's family situation was what one might call difficult. She lived in a small apartment with her parents and little sister. It wasn't always easy for my friend, but the difference in our family backgrounds didn't affect our friendship at all. When we were around fourteen, my friend's father announced that he was gay and that he was moving out to live with a man. That was really tough for her, not only at home but at school, because she dreaded the other students' reactions. I remember that our teacher made sure that we would all do our best to support her. Then we were both accepted into the same high school. Theoretically, we had the same chances of success because we had the same access to education and the same financial support, regardless of our family environment. But I say theoretically because in spite of it all, my friend dropped out of high school after a while. We lost touch so I don't know where she is now, but I am sure she's managed to find a path to a happy life. All this goes to show that even if a society offers everyone the same financial opportunities, it can't promise complete equality when it comes to success. The path may still be more difficult when you come from a disadvantaged background, or if psychological or emotional issues or simply a lack of support, information or prospects stop you from moving through the educational system.

DID YOU SAY MILLIONS?

But let's return to the American dream. If we interpret the American dream to mean becoming a millionaire, then we need to look elsewhere: Denmark is not the best place to get rich. There are many reasons for this: a tax system that redistributes earnings, as discussed; an education system that does not favor high achievers, as we've also seen; and quite simply that our culture does not put money first, which I'll come back to later. The fact remains that to become a millionaire in Denmark, you really need to have a revolutionary idea.

In 2011, sixty thousand Danes earned more than 1 million kroner ($151,000) out of a total population of 5.6 million.[4] I didn't find any reliable figures on what proportion of them already came from privileged backgrounds, but I can speak from experience: of the Danes I know who earn a lot of money, the vast majority of them come from Denmark's very large middle class or below. They all earn more than their parents.

To further my research, I contacted one of the biggest law firms in Copenhagen. The partners all earn more than one million kroner per year and are therefore members of the famous "1 percent." The partner who agreed to see me was from a working class background and grew up in a small town in Jutland.[5] We met in a beautiful meeting room in his magnificent offices overlooking the sea. He was very friendly, cheerful, down-to-earth and laid-back—the perfect embodiment of Denmark's unique social mobility. "If I'd been born in another country I don't think I'd be where I am today," he said, adding, "I had every opportunity to do what I wanted to do, regardless of where I started. I even managed to finish my law studies without going into debt, thanks to our grant system." He estimated that around 20 percent of the partners in the firm came from privileged backgrounds, but that the vast majority, about 60 percent, were from middle-class families. The remaining 20 percent came from genuinely challenging environments and had to fight a bit harder to overcome their tough socioeconomic background. "My motivation has never been to earn a lot of money, but to do something I love," the lawyer added with a smile. He did concede, however, that money gave him freedom and that he was proud and happy to pay very high taxes so he could give back to his country in exchange for everything he had received.

People often think that studying law at a university is mainly the preserve of students from privileged backgrounds or those who have a family tradition of going into the legal profession. But my interviewee estimated that only 30 percent of students in any given law school class are privileged, which means that the other 70 percent represent the full mix of social classes, with most coming from the middle classes. Of course, social mobility is still easier for middle-class people than for people from extremely underprivileged backgrounds, where there are more obstacles and greater difficulties despite the well-established and generous welfare system in Denmark.

But to reiterate, social mobility does not necessarily mean rising from the bottom upward, from poorer to richer. In the Danish sense, it primarily means having the opportunity to act independently of, and if necessary differently from, those who came before us. To act in a way that is true to ourselves. Remember Karen Blixen, the Danish heroine of the acclaimed film *Out of Africa*? Now, we can't say she came from nothing, because her family was very wealthy. But in her own way, she epitomizes this characteristically Danish belief in the ability to live your dream, even if it's dangerous or misunderstood. In the early twentieth century, Blixen rejected her bourgeois lifestyle and left Denmark to start a farm in Kenya. Her project was a financial failure, in the sense that she returned to Denmark with a lot less money than she had set out with—but she was much richer in terms of life experience, humanity and inspiration, which she shared with everyone who read her books.

Another perhaps more down-to-earth example is the taxi driver who took me to the airport when I was leaving Copenhagen recently after a weekend with my family. He told me his life story, as taxi drivers often do. "Well, you know, I used to wear a suit and tie every day and earn a lot of money. But one day I thought, why run around like this, just for status and material things?" He quit his job and had been working as a taxi driver for ten years. "I love the freedom you have in Denmark to choose the life you lead," he added. "I had everything I needed to go as far as I wanted, and now I choose to live more modestly, but calmly."

These are two typically Danish examples: no matter where you start out in life, all paths are possible.

REALISTIC EXPECTATIONS

I Have Realistic Dreams

> Danes love the simple things in life. They rarely
> have great ambitions of material wealth. They
> seldom dream of greatness or being the best;
> instead they simply take life as it comes.

Ever since I was little, I've gotten used to the following expressions: "with moderation" (*alt med måde*), "not so bad" (*ikke saa daarligt*) and "good enough" (*godt nok*). These sayings reflect a state of mind: it's going to be fine. And even if it's not the best, well, it's still okay. Having realistic expectations of life—and some would even say low expectations—is quite typical of the Danish mind-set.

KING CANUTE THE GREAT, CHAMPION OF EUROPE?

Apart from the Viking era, when Denmark was one of the biggest and most powerful countries in Europe (under King Canute the Great in the eleventh century, the kingdom of Denmark included Norway, vast territories of southern Sweden and much of England), we are not known for dreaming of national glory, nor for our need to be the best and beat everyone else. It's true that from the thirteen to the seventeenth centuries Denmark was a great world power with considerable influence. The kingdom conquered the shores of the Baltic and orchestrated Scandinavia's Kalmar Union, for example. But after this period there followed four centuries of unsuccessful battles and territory lost to the likes of Sweden, Norway, and the Prussian and Austrian armies in the nineteenth century, which all reduced the country to its current modest size. This history of greatness followed by dispossession has certainly contributed to the Danes' development of a realistic attitude toward life's difficulties.

You're probably wondering how this relates to happiness. The answer is simple: since we Danes don't expect to be the best, to win accolades or to be admired by others, we are more satisfied with the status quo. Then, if we are lucky enough to win something—or talented enough, though we usually don't brag about it too much—the pleasure is multiplied by a thousand. Usually, when we don't expect very much from a given situation, we're more likely to be pleasantly surprised in the end and therefore happier. Conversely, when we set the bar high, we often end up disappointed because things or people don't live up to our expectations.

Many European countries, such as Germany, England, France and Spain, have rich histories punctuated with numerous victories, long periods of greatness and periods of colonization around the world. The same goes for the United States, which has been a world superpower for a long time. Such cultures inevitably make it easier to dream of greatness, even from an individual perspective, but the constant drive to be the best undeniably leads to disappointment.

We can look for the origins of the Danes' realistic outlook in the country's past. Is it connected, perhaps, to the influence of Protestant culture, like our sense of independence? Protestantism took root very early on in Denmark, just as it did in the other Scandinavian countries. The Reformation reached Denmark in the 1520s, and when Christian III became king in 1536, Lutheranism became the official national religion of Denmark. Tensions remained, however, and there was plenty of back and forth between conservatives and reformers until religious freedom was finally enshrined by the Constitution of 1849. Nevertheless, Protestant culture made its mark on the Danish spirit, and today 5.6 million Danes (around 85 percent) are Christian, of which 4.5 million are Protestant. Catholicism today represents less than 1 percent of the population. Many major Danish historical figures were Protestant, including the sixteenth-century astronomer Tycho Brahe and famous authors such as Hans Christian Andersen, Karen Blixen and Søren Kierkegaard. This Protestant heritage, then, may be a contributing factor to our sense of realism. It is certainly the view put forward by acclaimed German economist and sociologist Max Weber in his book *The Protestant Ethic and the Spirit of Capitalism*.[1] According to Weber, Protestantism led to certain behaviors such as discipline and frugality, which in turn created a tendency to be content with little, not to spend too much and to work hard. Max Weber's thesis has been discussed at length, and it raises interesting questions about the origins of the Danes' realism.

FEET IN THE CLOUDS

In June 1992, hundreds of thousands of Danes took to the streets. The country was in the grip of euphoria: Denmark's football team had just won the European championship. Yet the team hadn't even qualified to begin with. The Danish team had been called up at the last minute to replace the Yugoslavian squad, which had been disqualified because of the war. Thousands of Danes with red-and-white painted faces had traveled to Sweden to support their team, while the rest were all glued to their TV sets. When the national anthem was played, you could hear the whole country singing *"Der er et yndigt land"* in the streets. How did our small country manage to beat the best teams in the tournament, such as Germany, France and the Netherlands?

This unexpected victory is a good illustration both of the way in which the unflappable Danes manage expectations (nobody had even dared entertain the idea of winning!) and of their modesty, which is part and parcel of their approach to life—and we'll return to this in another chapter.

This football triumph may have even been one of the happiest moments in the history of Denmark since the end of the Second World War. So much so that some experts who have tried to explain Danish happiness wonder whether this title, which is such a rarity for the Danes, still exerts an effect today.

The OECD created a Better Life Index that estimates life satisfaction, and guess what? Denmark is first (along with Iceland and Switzerland) with a satisfaction of 7.5/10 (the average grade is 6.6). In 2006,[2] a paper published in the *British Medical Journal* found the Danes to be the happiest people in Europe.[3] Citing the University of Leicester's World Map of Happiness and the annual Eurobarometer surveys, the authors reported that more than 66 percent of Danes claimed to be "very satisfied with their lives." The average for the other countries in Europe was 50 percent, with a significant proportion of countries hovering around 33 percent for the number of "very satisfied" citizens. Nothing new there, then, because as we already know, Denmark is almost always ranked as one of the most satisfied countries in the world. What *is* unique is the paper's conclusion that one of the main reasons for this satisfaction is the Danes' "low expectations."

But that's not all: the paper also offers a football-related explanation for Danish happiness. Looking back on Denmark's long series of unsuccessful wars, starting with a defeat in England in 1066, followed by the loss of Sweden, Norway, Northern Germany, the Danish West Indies and Iceland, it ends by stating that, other than our victory in the 1992 Euro Cup, we haven't won anything for centuries. The effect of this triumph could therefore still explain, at least in part, why the country is so satisfied. It's a persuasive conclusion, but since studies conducted before 1992 already found us to be the happiest country in the world, it is rather difficult to defend!

So let's put football aside and simply focus on the main thrust of the *British Medical Journal* paper: yes, expecting less makes you happier. But let's be clear—being a realist doesn't mean you don't have dreams or ideals. This is nicely explained by Tal Ben-Shahar, the Harvard positive psychology professor whose work we mentioned earlier. According to Ben-Shahar, contrasting realism (feet firmly on the ground) with idealism (head in the clouds) doesn't make sense. "Being an idealist is being a realist in the deepest sense—it is being true to our real nature,"[4] he explains, because "we are constituted so that we actually need our lives to have meaning." Without a final goal, a star to follow or a mountain to climb, we cannot fulfill our potential for happiness. This is not to imply that happiness means reaching the summit: being realistic means being able to enjoy the ascent, while acknowledging and accepting the obstacles along the way.

This "realistic idealism" has often helped me when facing difficult challenges. From an early age I dreamed of living in Paris, the capital of culture, gastronomy, philosophy and the art of living well—in short, the good life. But when I arrived in the City of Light at the age of eighteen, on my own, with just a basic knowledge of French and with only the Danish church as my point of reference, well, life wasn't as wonderful as I'd thought it would be. My idealism didn't desert me, though. I *wanted* to love Paris and I wanted Paris to love me back. But it was my realism that allowed me to withstand the long months of crying in the metro and of not understanding either the people or culture of this new country. I knew deep down that I was young and didn't have much life experience—I would have to fight for my happiness in Paris.

I was an au pair in a family with two little girls. I lived in a maid's room measuring just ten square meters (nearly eleven square feet) on the eighth floor of a building with no elevator. I worked from eight in the morning to eight at night. It was a far cry from my comfortable life in Denmark. After four months of crying a lot, my mother decided to drive all the way to Paris to take me home. She told me, "Darling, you've proved admirably that you are strong and brave, but there's no point in being so unhappy." I told her, "I knew this was going to be hard, but I'm following my dream and I'll decide whether or not to leave Paris when I'm happy here." She drove off in her car, leaving her "realistic idealist" daughter to make her own life.

Psychotherapist Sylvie Tenenbaum, in her book *C'est encore loin le bonheur? (How Far Off Is Happiness?),*[5] puts it this way: "There is an urgent need to renounce, once and for all, childhood and adolescence, illusions and impossible dreams: all they do is hinder the development of your personality, the fulfillment of all of your abilities that have lain dormant. . . . You need to be able to leave behind you all the things that inevitably distract you from accepting reality."

As a very wise, sensible friend told me one day when we were talking about our plans for the future and the changes we dreamed of making to our lives, "Whatever happens, life will always be a challenge, but every so often we just want to change what that challenge is!"

SOLIDARITY AND RESPECT FOR OTHERS

I Feel Better If You Feel Good

The vast majority of Danes are in favor of high taxes and are deeply committed to the welfare state. Sharing makes them happy, provided that everyone contributes.

Legend has it that at the height of the Second World War, King Christian X of Denmark rode through the streets of Copenhagen on horseback wearing a Star of David as a mark of solidarity with the Jews.

In actual fact, there are no photos or sources to confirm this heroic act. Moreover, Danish Jews were never forced to wear the Star of David. The legend seems to have originated from a telegram published in London in 1942: "When the Danish king learned that the Germans wanted to force [Jews] to wear a yellow Star of David, he declared, 'If this happens, I will pin it to my own uniform and will order my retinue to do the same.'" Although it is an apocryphal story, it demonstrates something important nonetheless: that solidarity is a typical characteristic of our mentality and culture, not only among Danes, but in relation to the outside world. With or without a Star of David-wearing king, the Danes did all they could to protect the Jews during the war. The Danish Resistance notably organized a rescue operation in which fishermen ferried some seventy-two hundred Jews (out of a total population of seventy-eight hundred) to safe haven in Sweden, a neutral country.[1] The Danish Underground is the only group in the world to have been collectively commemorated on the "Righteous among the Nations" list drawn up by Yad Vashem. The same honor has been bestowed on more than twenty-five thousand individuals for exceptional acts of courage, generosity and humanity.[2]

TAX FATIGUE?

Proof of this national solidarity can be found in the Danes' massive support for our tax system. One 2012 survey involving more than two thousand Danes confirms their commitment to the welfare state and their willingness to fund it through taxation.[3] Seven out of ten Danes were happy with the balance between taxes paid and services provided by the State. For those with the lowest incomes, who earn less than 200,000 kroner ($30,000) per year, this figure rises to more than 80 percent. It falls to 40 percent among those with incomes of more than a million kroner ($151,000) per year, who represent little more than 1 percent of the population.[4]

The tax revenue as a percentage of GDP in Denmark is the highest in the world at 50.9 percent, compared with the OECD country average of 34.4 percent (total tax revenue in France stood at around 45.2 percent of GDP in 2014 according to the OECD, the second highest of all OECD countries). The United Kingdom is a bit below average at 33.1 percent, whereas the

United States is among the lowest at only 26.0 percent (Mexico has a lower rate at 19.5 percent).[5]

The marginal tax rate of 56.2 percent in Denmark, also one of the highest in Europe, is applied to earnings of more than 467,400 kroner ($70,900) per year, whereas the average Danish income is 294,000 kroner ($44,600) per year.[6] According to the Danish Tax Ministry, the marginal tax rate is paid by 14 percent of the population.

Yet despite this high rate of taxation, no one suffers from tax fatigue in Denmark. Only 20 percent of Danes think they pay too much tax, compared with 66 percent who feel that the rate of taxation is fair, and 12 percent who believe that they don't pay enough![7] This is indicative of the trust they have in their government to put tax revenue to good use for public services, education, health and transportation infrastructure. Sixty-one percent of Danes even claim that they wouldn't care if their taxes were lowered.

My French bank manager called me one day. "Madame Rydahl, I need to see you urgently!"

I was quite taken aback, because I've always had a good relationship with my bank and I am very good at managing my money. I replied, "Why, what's the problem?"

She responded in a very serious voice, "I've noticed that you're paying way too much in taxes. I've got some ideas on how to pay a lot less."

"Really?" I asked, surprised. "But my tax return is pretty straightforward, so I don't think . . ."

"On the contrary, Madame Rydahl," she insisted. "You see, if you buy property on some offshore islands and . . ."

I interrupted her. "That's very sweet of you, but you know, I'm very happy to live in France and it's my pleasure to contribute to the social security system by paying taxes—even high ones!"

She fell silent for a moment, then recovered. "You're very funny, Madame Rydahl! People have played a lot of jokes on me but never one this good!"

As this anecdote illustrates, my attitude is not necessarily shared by the rest of Europe or the world—far from it. In France, for example, nearly three-quarters of the population (72 percent) think they pay too much in taxes. Seventy-four percent also believe that they contribute more to the system than they get out of it. Eighty-eight percent of French people think that tax revenue is poorly utilized by the government. And almost half (45 percent) approve of those who decide to move abroad to pay less in taxes.[8] In Spain, nine out of ten people believe that taxes are not collected fairly. Almost 67 percent of them also think that the State gives them less in return than they pay in taxes and contributions, and 70 percent feel that on the whole, citizens get little or less than they give in taxes.[9] Taxation is also a controversial issue in the United States. The U.S. tax system is quite unique in that it is based on citizenship rather than country of residence, which means that no matter where an American lives and earns their money, they must file a tax return with the Internal Revenue Service. If the amount of tax paid in their country of residence is lower than their U.S. tax bill, they must pay the difference to the IRS.[10] Recent changes to U.S. fiscal policy have raised the tax burden and given the IRS more power to pursue individuals and corporations so that U.S. expatriates don't get away with tax avoidance. The result is that more and more Americans are choosing to give up their citizenship. According to statistics published in the *Federal Register* (the daily journal of the U.S. government), 4,279 Americans relinquished their citizenship in 2015, whereas there were "only" 1,781 in 2011.[11] While this figure may seem insignificant given that there are five million Americans living abroad, it is still fourteen times higher than in 2006 (when no more than 300 tore up their passports). This is a fast-growing trend.

A few weeks after the conversation with my bank manager, I was having dinner at a friend's house. In the middle of the meal, my friend's husband, a successful businessman, announced, "Well I've never paid a centime of taxes in France. Quite honestly I don't agree with it, seeing as the politicians are so useless."

Not wishing to get into a heated debate, I said simply, "But you've earned a lot of money for years—I didn't even know it was possible not to pay anything."

"Oh yes," he replied proudly, "there's always a way if you really don't want to pay. Frankly, if the money is going to be spent like that, I don't want to be a part of it."

I looked at him, intrigued by his logic. "Okay, I know that things like the rate of taxation and politics are obviously up for discussion, but don't you feel it's your duty to contribute at least a little bit? After all, you benefit from the infrastructure, hospitals, police, the legal system—that's worth some contribution, isn't it?"

Looking a little embarrassed, he changed the subject. "Let's talk about something else. I went to see an exhibition organized by the City Hall the other day. It was wonderful, and it's completely free!"

SOLIDARITY AND FAIR PLAY

Let's be clear: the Danes are happy to share, provided that everyone contributes and respects the system without trying to freeload or cheat.

Let's go back to 2011. The election campaign in Denmark was in full swing. Özlem Cekic, a spokesperson for the left-wing Socialist People's Party (SF), wanted to prove that poverty did exist, even in Denmark. She decided to take up the case of Carina, an unemployed single mother who, she said, was having trouble making ends meet. But on closer inspection, it turned out that Carina was getting a net total of almost 16,000 kroner ($2,400) per month in benefits. After paying all her expenses, including buying cigarettes, she still had 5,000 kroner ($754) in disposable income. The case caused a scandal. "Poor Carina" earned more in benefits than people who worked! The media had a field day and Danes were outraged. They were happy to pay high taxes and contribute to a socially cohesive system, but they didn't want to be taken for fools. However, a survey conducted after this episode showed that the "Carina effect" was actually fairly limited.[12] There was only a small increase in those who thought social security benefits were too high (from 24 percent to 28 percent), while almost 60 percent of Danes still believed the amount of benefits was fair, or even not enough.

This notion of respect for others, as long as they actively contribute to society, is essential. The last socialist government (2011–2015) has made it a key issue. Its ethos: differentiating between those who can but don't want to, and those who want to but can't. A new reform replaced unemployment benefits for young people under the age of thirty with a financial support scheme using student grants. Furthermore, anyone who receives benefits and is able to work must also contribute to their local community by taking part in activities that benefit everyone (cleaning the streets, parks and beaches, helping the elderly, etc.). According to one study, 80 percent of Danes supported this initiative.[13] More generally, this reform also imposed tougher conditions on people receiving unemployment benefits. They must demonstrate that they are actively seeking employment by sending a certain number of job applications per week and posting them on the site jobnet.dk, so that the job center manager can follow their job search. Unemployed people who fail to attend an interview, refuse a job that would be suitable for them or do not appear to be actively seeking employment will have their benefits reconsidered.[14]

While it's true that the unemployment benefit system is quite generous (particularly for union members), it requires payment of an insurance premium each month. On average, unemployed people in Denmark receive around 73 percent of their former earnings during the first four years of unemployment compensation. Compare that with 33 percent in the United Kingdom; around 65 percent in Spain for the first two years, then 25 percent for the next two; 67 percent in Germany, which progressively falls year after year to 37 percent; and 67 percent in France for the first two years, followed by 30 percent for the next two.[15] In the United States, the unemployment benefits are around 40–50 percent of one's salary, but only for a period of six months. After that, if the person has not found a job, there is no further financial support from the government.[16] However, very high earners in Denmark can't rely on unemployment benefits because the maximum benefit is fixed at 16,000 kroner ($2,400) gross per month, whatever the original salary. But at the end of the day, relying on unemployment benefits is not something that sits well with Danish culture; as we have already seen in the case of "Lazy Robert," everyone must contribute to ensure a fair and equal society.

A few years ago I went through a period of soul-searching about my career. In 2003, after my mentor Elisabeth's departure from Bang & Olufsen, I found myself in a very different world: that of advertising. I hadn't really chosen the job, but it paid the bills. I had taken the position of account manager for a major Parisian department store. Having gotten used to Elisabeth's management style, this experience was a great opportunity to immerse myself in a new and very different environment—an advertising agency that was not just French but very Parisian. The first day, one of the directors took me aside to tell me about the client we would be meeting the next day. "Er, how should I put this?" he began. "Tomorrow you'll be meeting the directors of our agency's most important client."

I smiled at him happily and replied, "Yes, I'm looking forward to it!"

A little embarrassed, he continued, "So, just to make sure it goes well, do you think you could avoid looking too 'Right Bank'? I mean, don't take this the wrong way, but you know, Left Bank people are more comfortable with a very discreet, understated look."

The question of which side of the Seine I came from had never occurred to me before, so I tried to figure out what he was getting at. "If I understand you correctly, you're worried that my appearance will upset the client to the point that the meeting could go badly?" He didn't reply, and I continued, "Listen, I'm

Danish, so by definition I'm neither Right Bank nor Left Bank. If it makes you happy, I can dress like I'm from the Île Saint-Louis since it is right in the centre of the river. In any case, I think I'm prepared to take the risk of my physical appearance not being liked. If that's how this works, I might as well give up right now!" In the end, no one was offended by my physical appearance and this job taught me a lot about creativity, human relationships and my own limitations. It also taught me that it wasn't the right career path to follow for my own personal fulfillment.

I decided to talk to a few friends and ask for their advice. "You know, I'm not really happy at work. It's not the right career for me and I think I need to change direction."

My friends all unanimously replied, "Yes, Malene, you're right, it's better to make a change if you're not happy. Life's too short."

I was pleased they supported me. Then I said, "I know I'm going to find something else, but it's going to be hard while I'm working. I don't have a choice, though, because I have to pay my rent."

They all looked at me with surprise: "What are you talking about? Just negotiate the end of your contract, sign up for unemployment, and take your time to think about things." I obviously got the idea—as it seemed absurd to negotiate the end of my contract when I was the one who had decided to leave—that it seemed crazy to receive employment benefits while I was just "thinking about" my career, when that thinking time would be funded by other people's hard work.

There's a term that perfectly expresses this attitude of generosity combined with accountability: our famous Danish "flexicurity." While unemployment benefits in Denmark are, admittedly, quite high, they also go together with well-defined policies to encourage job seekers, as well as low job protection. This means it is easier and less expensive to let go of an employee in Denmark than in many other European countries, but it is also easier to find a new job quickly and to be supported during the transition period, which is shorter. In 2012, according to the OECD, "only" 28 percent of jobless Danes were unemployed long term (that is, for more than a year). We could do better. Some countries are well ahead of us (8 percent in Norway and 17.5 percent in Sweden, whose systems are also based on the flexicurity model; 20 percent in Australia and 13 percent in New Zealand), although other nations unfortunately reported much higher rates of long-term unemployment as a percentage of the total number of unemployed (30 percent in the United States, 35 percent in the United Kingdom, 39 percent in Japan, 40 percent in France, 45 percent in Spain, 47 percent in Germany and 53 percent in Italy).[17]

Taxes are also used to fund completely free medical coverage for the whole population. This essential element clearly provides Danes with a great sense of security. But good health doesn't necessarily make us happier in our everyday lives, because people get used to "feeling good" when they wake up. This is why it's often said that people who have been ill enjoy life even more—they don't take good health for granted.

Solidarity is also expressed through tolerance and open-mindedness toward minorities in society. In 1989, Denmark became the first country in the world to allow gay couples the right to an "officially registered partnership." In 2010 the right for couples in a registered partnership to adopt children was passed. The Danish Protestant church also allows priests to

hold religious ceremonies for gay couples. The vast majority of
the Danish population is in favor of this: according to a survey
by Capacent Research for *Kristeligt Dagblad*, a leading Christian
newspaper in Denmark, 63 percent support these measures and
only 25 percent are against. In 2012 a new law was passed that
officially makes marriage gender neutral.

The debate over immigration in Denmark is more complex.
The "new Danes" (*ny dansker*) now represent around 10 percent
of the Danish population, and their integration remains a
contentious issue. The far-right Danish People's Party (Dansk
Folkeparti) obtained 12.3 percent of the votes in the last legis-
lative elections, yet the Danes are usually known for their tolerance to minorities. So how do you explain the support for
this political party? According to Professor Christian Bjørnskov, this negative perception of immigrants is mainly due to
the image the media has created of new Danes who supposedly
abuse the social security system. It's true that immigrants are
more often in precarious economic situations, and according to
a 2010 survey conducted by the Economic Council of the Labour
Movement (ECLM), a Danish economic policy institute and
think tank, one out of six new Danes is unemployed, compared
with one in eighteen for the rest of the population. This doesn't
mean, however, that statistically they take more advantage of
the system. The far right regularly fuels the debate with negative cases reported by the press, along the lines of "better to
help people where they are rather than letting them come to
Denmark." And Danish tolerance wears thin if they fear that
their shared national project and the welfare state are being
threatened. The Danes' trust in one another and in their institutions is very high, as we've seen, which makes cheating or

abusing the system all the more intolerable, whether the perpetrators are new Danes or the rest of the population.

FROM RED LIGHTS TO THE BALLOT BOX

Beyond solidarity, the Danes feel truly responsible for a shared national project. But for this project to succeed, it is crucial to respect the rules and show a certain sense of civic-mindedness in society.

It was the middle of the night in November 1997. I was a student in Copenhagen and walking home after a get-together with some friends. It was cold and raining. I'd forgotten my umbrella and was completely soaked. Although there wasn't a soul in the streets, I stopped at every red light and waited for the walk signal to turn green. At the last light, I crossed someone's path. He gave me a puzzled look as I waited patiently, wet and freezing. "Why on earth aren't you crossing the road?" he asked. "There hasn't been a single car for an hour!"

But my attitude was typically Danish. You hardly ever see a Dane cross the road when the light is red: it would be so frowned upon that someone would no doubt say something, not to mention the threat of a 500-kroner ($75) fine. The same goes if you litter. These principles are so ingrained in our culture that even after nineteen years in France, I still have trouble crossing against the light. I do it anyway, but each time I'm very conscious of what I'm doing. My friends think it's funny and I can understand why—ever since they were children, they've checked both ways and if there aren't any cars coming, they just go ahead and cross!

Yet again, what matters in Denmark is that the individual's

high standards reflect society's high standards. This is probably why voter turnout is so high in Denmark. It rose to 86 percent in the last elections, higher than the OECD average of 68 percent. (The figure stood at 81 percent for the second round of the 2012 presidential elections in France.)[18] In Denmark, 90 percent of the wealthiest 20 percent of the population votes, as does 86 percent of the poorest 20 percent. This difference in voter turnout (four percentage points) is lower than the OECD average, where there is a gap of twelve percentage points between the wealthiest and poorest voters.[19] Proof that nearly everyone fulfills their civic duty. In Denmark, happiness only counts if it's shared by everyone.

WORK–LIFE BALANCE

I Want Lots of *Hygge* Time

Family and leisure are an important part of
Danish life. Danes leave work by 5 p.m. to spend
time with their children.

n 2010, then Danish prime minister Lars Løkke Rasmussen
was caught up in a media storm. He had just canceled a meeting with eighty international diplomats for what he referred
to as personal reasons. Rumors started flying around. People
were saying he'd stayed home to look after his daughter, who
had sprained her ankle. The situation became so tense that
Rasmussen had to hold a press conference. He denied the story
about his daughter, but made it very clear that while he took the
role of prime minister extremely seriously it was only a tempo-
rary role, whereas he was a father for life. Soon after, he went
on vacation with his family before the school term had ended
so he could spend time with them, even though the rules say he
should respect the school terms.

In Denmark people value their work–life balance to such an
extent that the Rasmussen incident ultimately had a positive
effect on his relationship with voters. The Danes liked the fact
that the man running our country was a man of principle who

put his family first. They felt he had spoken honestly and that his values reflected their own.

MORE FREE TIME MEANS HAPPIER PEOPLE

According to the latest research by the OECD,[1] Denmark has achieved the best work–life balance of all members of the organization, along with Spain. On average, Danes devote 69 percent of their day to personal activities. This represents just over sixteen hours, compared with the OECD average of fifteen hours. France is ranked sixth, the United Kingdom twenty-fourth and the United States thirty-second out of thirty-six countries, with Canada, Poland, Mexico and Turkey bringing up the rear. Only 2 percent of employees in Denmark work longer than normal hours, whereas the OECD average is 9 percent.

The Danish social and professional system is designed to facilitate this balance. For example, Danish employees are entitled to five weeks' paid vacation per year, as in many other European countries. But if one of their children falls ill, parents get even more time off: they can stay at home with their child for one day without counting it as leave.

The balance between work and leisure is also reflected in our flexible working hours. One Dane in four feels comfortable tailoring their work schedule around their daily routine in order to create a balanced life. A significant proportion of the working population (17 percent) even does some part of their work from home so they can look after their family more easily.[2] Danish companies have a very progressive attitude toward this behavior, and no one bats an eyelid if a parent leaves work at 4 p.m. to pick their children up from day care.

My closest Danish girlfriends with children have all adopted this system so they can be there for their little ones during those crucial early years. They have negotiated flexible working hours that enable them to leave early to spend time with their family. One of my friends who is recently divorced even takes her children to the office after picking them up so she can finish her work in peace. (Although I'm not sure how peaceful it really is with a four-year-old girl and a two-year-old boy in the office!) And fathers are equally involved, of course. They are often the ones who leave work early to pick up their children at 5 p.m.

You may be thinking, *Okay, that's all well and good, but what about people in positions of responsibility who need to be present at the office?* The Danish association Lederne (meaning "Leaders"), a nonpolitical federation for managers and executives, carried out a survey on work–life balance among 1,585 of its 100,000 members.[3] The result, unsurprisingly, was that a person's level of responsibility affects their work–life balance. Six out of ten executives admitted that their workload sometimes required them to work at home during the evenings and weekends. That said, three out of four still believed they were in control of how their working day was organized and eight out of ten said they felt free to arrange daytime visits to the doctor or dentist. Fifty percent reported even being able to deal with personal matters during work time. In total, 85 percent of those who took part in the survey said they were satisfied or very satisfied with their working conditions, and two-thirds were satisfied with their work–life balance. Only one in ten claimed to be very dissatisfied. Of the third who were not satisfied with their work–life balance, more than half said they were thinking of changing jobs to find a better compromise.

Even though we seem to be more progressive on this front than many other countries, clearly some families live with the stress of being single-parent households and are therefore unable to achieve the same balance in all aspects of their life. But the Lederne survey confirms that Danes are very aware of the importance of work–life balance and if they don't think their situation is working for them, they feel free to change it.

PEDALING THROUGH LIFE!

Balancing work and personal time also comes down to practicalities. For instance, experts have noted that the time spent traveling to and from work is an important factor in overall life satisfaction. When it comes to commuting the Danes again rank very high, with an average of just twenty-seven minutes' travel time per day compared with thirty-eight minutes on average for other OECD countries.[4] And since their preferred mode of transport is the bicycle, this gives them even more flexibility because they don't have to worry about traffic or parking. On average, Danes between ten and eighty-four years old cycle 0.47 times per day (which means they ride their bikes roughly every other day) and 46 percent use bikes as their primary mode of transportation to work, school or a university.[5] In Copenhagen, the figure is even higher, with 50 percent of the population getting on their bikes whatever the occasion. When I go out with my girlfriends there, they all turn up in little dresses and heels—on bicycles! Even in December and when it's raining. It's also important to point out that those who choose to cycle are not doing so to save money, because people from all economic backgrounds ride bikes. Even politicians pedal: 63 percent of

Danish members of parliament travel to Christianborg (the seat of Parliament) by bike.[6]

FROM HOME SWEET HOME . . .

So what do the Danes do with all this free time?

Rush hour in Denmark is from 4 to 5 p.m. People are leaving work either to pick up their children or simply to do the things they enjoy. Family and leisure time in general are very important to the Danes. They eat dinner around 6 p.m., and the whole family dines together, in contrast with certain other cultures where the children eat first and the parents later, or where everyone eats on their own.

One of my favorite Danish words is *hygge*. It's a difficult concept to explain, because there is no real equivalent in other languages. Essentially, it describes something warm and intimate. Danes use the word in lots of situations and always in a very positive sense. *Hygge* is also closely connected to social occasions with family and friends—for example, having dinner or sharing a few beers in a warm, friendly atmosphere filled with candlelight. December is the most "*hyggelig*" month in Denmark: everywhere is illuminated by millions of candles and people get together to drink mulled wine and listen to Christmas carols. It's quite magical. Candles are almost always part of *hygge* time.

The term "*hygge*" is so important to our culture that one social anthropologist, Jeppe Trolle Linnet of the University of Southern Denmark, has even specialized in the study of the phenomenon. He explains that *hygge* is something all Danes share, a kind of expression of our unity. He also notes that the context may vary depending on the social setting, but that no matter how it happens, it usually includes eating and drinking. Linnet has made another observation that may surprise non-Danes: most Danes have trouble experiencing the *hygge* spirit if the setting or atmosphere is too luxurious.[7] This is in keeping with the values we have already discussed—namely, a certain level of modesty and reserve when it comes to luxury and ostentation. *Hygge* must be simple and accessible to all. In other words, if you want to create some Danish *hygge*, don't bother with the champagne and caviar.

A sense of *hygge* can also be found in our world-famous Scandinavian design, to which Danish architects and designers such as Arne Jacobsen and Verner Panton have contributed. Home interiors are welcoming, comfortable and beautiful, but not in the luxurious sense. It is a simple beauty that makes you feel good, featuring natural materials, clean lines and practical design. Of course, not everybody can live in designer homes (although Swedish brand Ikea has set out to make designer furniture more affordable), but the concept of a beautiful, functional interior that is friendly and uplifting is part and parcel of *hygge*.

When I was a child, my mother would make us a fire in the hearth every evening and light candles all around the house. After dinner it was *hygge* time, when we would watch films or play board games. I was lucky enough to have had a childhood filled with love and lots of *hygge* time.

But let's be clear: despite *hygge* and all that free time to spend on ourselves, our friends and family, things aren't always perfect even in the best of worlds. Leisure time in Denmark can also degenerate into unhappy situations, such as alcohol abuse.

We can't ignore the issue: alcohol consumption challenges this idea of Danish happiness.

I remember going to a party at my secondary school when I was around sixteen. It was awful right from the start because it was a costume party and I hated dressing up. Then, even though we were under the teachers' supervision (which is not to say we had their blessing), it turned into a massive party with plenty of booze. I'm not proud of myself, but I wasn't used to drinking and didn't have the stomach for it, and by the end of the evening I found I couldn't stand up, let alone get myself home after the party. At that point a taxi pulled up and the driver kindly offered, indeed not to take me home, but to the hospital! Unfortunately, Danish hospital staff are used to seeing young people in this state, but I was so ashamed at the thought of my parents finding out and coming to pick me up from the hospital that I begged my girlfriends to get me out of there. They effectively "kidnapped" me, getting down on all fours to carry me out of the hospital. Clearly this wasn't my finest hour as a teenager in Aarhus. But luckily for me, the experience didn't end very badly—I just had a terrible headache the next day.

In Denmark it's also common for young people to get together at home before a night out for a so-called warm-up (*opvarming*). The idea is to drink as much alcohol as possible so you're already plastered when you hit the bars and clubs. I had a lot of fun (and quite a few headaches), but it's not exactly the healthiest tradition for young Danes.

Of course, young people are not the only ones who drink. According to the European School Survey Project on Alcohol and Other Drugs (ESPAD), an average of 79 percent of European teenagers ages fifteen and sixteen admit to having consumed at least one alcoholic drink in the past twelve months, and the "regular" use of alcohol among fifteen- to sixteen-year-olds ("regular" being defined as at least ten occasions within the past thirty days) varies between 79 percent of young people in the Czech Republic and 17 percent in Iceland. Denmark's young people rank second highest in regular alcohol consumption, with 76 percent claiming to have drunk alcohol within the past thirty days, followed by Germany at 73 percent, Greece at 72 percent and Cyprus at 70 percent. France comes in at 67 percent, Italy at 63 percent and the United Kingdom at 65 percent.[8] And Denmark's teens top the charts (along with Malta) in terms of "heavy episodic drinking within the past thirty days" (that is, having five or more drinks on one occasion), at 56 percent—well above the ESPAD average of 39 percent. In the United States, meanwhile, the 2011 National Survey on Drug Use and Health found that 25 percent of young people ages twelve to twenty drank alcohol and 16 percent of them reported binge drinking, in spite of the fact that the legal drinking age is twenty-one.[9] And in Russia, another study observed that as many as 80 percent of young Russians consume alcoholic drinks.[10] Whatever the story in other countries, alcohol consumption among Danish teenagers continues to be a concerning problem and Denmark ranks highest in Europe when it comes to the proportion of young people who claim already to have been drunk at some point in their lives (85 percent).[11]

It's hard to establish a direct link between levels of alcohol consumption and happiness. Consuming too much alcohol may be the expression of unhappiness, but that's not its only function. Alcohol is also part of culture and society's traditions, not just in Denmark but in many other countries including

France and the United Kingdom. In Denmark, alcohol plays an important role in our social gatherings and traditions. If someone says no when offered a drink, it's not always well received, because to a Dane's way of thinking it smacks of unfriendliness.

But this isn't simply a moral issue, and you can't unravel a subject as complex as the whys and wherefores of alcohol consumption in a few short lines.

The freedom to balance your career with your personal life, family and friends is clearly a key factor in Danish happiness. But the joys of *hygge* must sometimes be consumed in moderation.

. . . TO OUR HOMELAND

In Denmark, being together is not just about being with your private circle of family and friends. It has a much wider sense that encompasses society as a whole. Danes' sense of belonging to "one big family" that cultivates *hygge* is reflected in the love they have for their country, its symbols and values. For example, we are very fond of the *Dannebro* our flag. It not only symbolizes the country itself, but all our festivals and celebrations. The Danish flag is omnipresent at birthday parties; indeed, a birthday card is not a birthday card without a drawing of the flag. And in the vast majority of Danish gardens, you'll see the flag flying at the top of a flagpole for any occasion. Even at Christmas we decorate our trees with little flags. To help you visualize this better, I should add that Danes like to dance around the Christmas tree while holding hands and singing Christmas carols (we may be the only people in the world who do this).

Speaking of Christmas, can you guess what the most popular Christmas present is in Denmark? The answer often surprises people: underwear. That's right—underpants, and no doubt socks—are very commonly exchanged as gifts between family and friends. I actually conducted a little survey of my own among my Danish friends and the results speak volumes. They were all well aware of this phenomenon and openly admitted that underpants and socks were classic gifts. One of my girlfriends also mentioned other interesting presents, such as the broom she had given her husband, and the nose hair trimmer her mother-in-law had bought her father, which is another classic that appears under many a Danish Christmas tree every year (though they're hardly at the top of anyone's wish list). Potato peelers and garlic presses are also top choices.

The year I turned fifteen I went Christmas shopping with my father. The Danish tradition of very practical and quite unexciting gifts always made us laugh a lot, so we decided to go all-out: reindeer-patterned boxers for my grandfather, big woolly underpants for my aunt, anti-odor foot cream for my cousin, a 1.5-quart bottle of pine-scented cologne for my uncle, mouthwash for my other cousin—you get the idea. Against all odds, the gifts were a great success. As my uncle said, "It's great, all this stuff is so practical!"

Of course, every country has traditions and festivals that unite its people, and Denmark is hardly unique in this respect. But what's certain is that Danes spend more time together. Sixty percent of Europeans spend time with their family, friends and relations at least once a week, whereas among the Danes the figure is 78 percent.[12]

This widespread sense of family is also seen in the affection

Danes have for their royal family. Although this may seem surprising in a country as egalitarian as Denmark, the royal family is very popular with the people. The monarchs embody the country's unity. There is overwhelming support for them, with 77 percent of Danes in favor of the monarchy, as opposed to only 16 percent who would prefer a republic. This is much higher than in other European monarchies, where the average level of support is around 58 percent.[13]

Danes also love gathering in associations. The saying goes that if you put three Danes in the same room, they will form a club. That may be an exaggeration, but the fact remains that Danes have managed to found more than one hundred thousand volunteer associations and organizations of all kinds.[14] The estimated value of the volunteer sector in Denmark is as much as 135 billion kroner ($20 billion) per year, roughly 10 percent of Denmark's GDP. Denmark devotes more time to volunteer work than any other European country,[15] ahead of Finland, Sweden, Austria and the Netherlands. But other countries are also recognized world leaders in this sector, notably the United States: according to U.S. federal government statistics, almost a fifth of the population (more than sixty-two million Americans) volunteer every year, dedicating over eight billion hours of service valued at $173 billion.[16]

I distinctly remember my father being a very active member of a number of sports associations when I was a child. He was passionate about all sports and even played for the Danish national handball team, scoring thirty-four goals in twenty-five matches. I'd say he spent close to 25 percent of his time volunteering, particularly in the sports sector. My mother also belonged to a lot of associations when she was younger. Like my father, she had been a Scout for several years and even formed her own bowling association. And for the record, my parents actually met at a party organized by the Aarhus handball association. Without these associations, I wouldn't be here today talking to you about Danish happiness.

As for me, I can't claim to have made a particularly impressive effort in volunteering because I left my country at eighteen. However, for several years at Christmastime I would dress up as an elf and go to the local retirement homes playing Christmas carols on my recorder. I don't think my performance was particularly impressive, but as quite a few members of my audience were hard of hearing, I was still very well received!

In short, I believe that being able to devote time to your family and friends, as well as to the associations and community causes you believe in, is another key factor in Danish happiness.

RELATIONSHIP TO MONEY
I'm Happy with What I've Got

Danes are generally quite relaxed when it comes
to money. For most, being rich is not a priority.

Once upon a time a businessman was sitting on the beach
in a Brazilian village. He saw a fisherman rowing toward
the shore with a boat full of big fish. Impressed, the
businessman asked the fisherman, "How long did it take you to
catch all those fish?"

"Oh, not long at all," replied the fisherman.

"So why didn't you stay at sea longer to catch even more?"
asked the businessman with surprise.

"This is enough to feed my whole family," explained the fisherman calmly.

"But what are you going to do for the rest of the day?" continued the businessman.

"Well," said the fisherman, "I wake up early in the morning,
go to sea to catch some fish, then come home to play with my
children. In the afternoon I take a siesta with my wife and in
the evening I meet my friends in the village for a drink, and we
sing and dance and play the guitar all night long."

The businessman thought for a moment, then made a suggestion to the fisherman: "I have an MBA. I could help you become a lot richer. You'll have to spend a lot more time at sea and try to catch as many fish as possible. When you've saved enough money you'll be able to buy a bigger boat and catch even more fish. Then you'll be able to buy more boats, and set up your own company and your own fish processing factory and distribution network. By this time you'll have left this village and moved to São Paulo, where you'll base your headquarters so you can manage the other branches of your company."

The fisherman shook his head. "And after that?"

"After that," laughed the businessman, "you'll be able to live like a king, and once you've made a name for yourself you can start trading on the stock market, and you'll become very rich."

"And after that?" asked the fisherman again.

"After that," continued the businessman, "you'll finally be able to retire, move away, and buy a little house in a fishing village, where you'll wake up early in the morning, catch a few fish, go home to play with your children, take a lovely siesta with your wife, meet your friends for a drink in the evening, and sing and dance and play the guitar all night long!"

To which the fisherman, perplexed, replied, "But isn't that exactly what I'm doing now?"

LOW ON DOUGH OR GLUTEN-FREE?

I love that story. In its way it perfectly illustrates the Danish mentality: Danes are generally quite relaxed when it comes to money. This may be because a good dose of *hygge* time makes them happier than a big salary, as we've already seen. It may also be because they know the welfare state will cover their basic needs and there's no risk of being left without life's essentials. For most Danes, being rich is not a priority.

When I went back to my old school in Aarhus, Skaade Skole, to speak to the ninth-year students (ages fifteen to sixteen), we also discussed this attitude toward money. Most of them came from privileged backgrounds and I wanted to hear their opinions on the subject. Only one student thought earning a lot of money was important. However, she did clarify that she wanted to earn a lot of money doing a job she loved. The rest unanimously preferred the idea of finding a job that was both meaningful and enjoyable. Of course, you may say that by framing the question the way I did, no one would have been brave enough to honestly respond, "No, I just want to be rich at the expense of my happiness." That being said, whenever I hear and observe Danes, they don't give me the impression of being caught up in the rat race for money. In a certain sense they already consider themselves very rich, or at least privileged, because of their social welfare system. And as we have seen, they have other priorities such as achieving a good work–life balance, solidarity and personal fulfillment.

The young people I interviewed would no doubt identify with the ideas of the late British philosopher and writer Alan Watts, who did a lot of work on the pursuit of happiness and was influenced by Eastern and Western spiritual teachings. Watts's main conclusions are summed up in a popular YouTube video called *What If Money Was No Object?*[1] His message is clear: find out what you really want to do and do it, whether it promises to make you rich or not, because any other path will lead to an unfulfilling and poor life. "Why spend your life making money doing things you don't like doing, in order to go on living, doing things you don't like doing?" asks Watts. If you want to be happy, the most important thing is to discover what you are passionate about and have the courage to follow this path.

In much the same way, when I was working at the advertising agency and went through a period of soul-searching about my career, I wanted to get back to basics. I wanted to find out what I was really passionate about so that I could be true to myself and feel happy every morning when I went to work. I asked myself lots of questions. I revisited my childhood dream: the hotel industry. I was well aware that it wasn't common to change careers in the French system. But I told myself that I didn't have a choice, because sometimes the greatest risk you can take is not to take one. I started contacting some of Paris's beautiful luxury hotels. One day I met an absolutely wonderful woman in a magnificent hotel on Place de la Concorde. I was captivated by her personality and wanted to work for her at all costs. I went so far as to offer to take a 40 percent pay cut to follow my dream. Although we really hit it off, she turned down my proposal, saying, "I really like you, but money always ends up influencing us and you'll resent me in six months' time when you're at the office at 8 o'clock, it's raining, and you can't afford to take a taxi or go to a restaurant like you could before." I disagreed, even though I think her theory was based on her rich life experiences, whereas mine was perhaps based on my lack of experience. Whatever the case, I still wanted to work in the hotel industry, no matter the salary prospects. In the summer of 2005, I was eventually hired as the communications director of Relais & Châteaux, the international chain of luxury boutique hotels.

This relates back to what I discussed earlier regarding independence: Danish happiness comes first and foremost from our ability to express fully who we are. It's no coincidence that this idea is found throughout the work of one of our most famous thinkers, Søren Kierkegaard, the nineteenth-century philosopher, theologian and poet. Kierkegaard's philosophy is extremely rich and complex, but contains a common thread: How do we become human, and how do we become ourselves? He believed that the duty of the individual was to understand himself and follow his own vocation: "One must learn to know oneself before knowing anything else," he wrote. "Not until a person has inwardly understood himself and then sees the course he is to take does his life gain peace and meaning. . . . What matters is to find a purpose . . . the crucial thing is to find a truth that is true for me, to find the idea for which I am willing to live and die."[2] In this sense, many Danes live Kierkegaard's philosophy without necessarily knowing it: they attach more importance to carving out their own way in life than to building their investment portfolio.

My brother Jesper is a good example of someone who has followed this philosophy. During his first year at Copenhagen Business School, where he studied international marketing and management, he had an internship at one of the best web design studios in Denmark, which would lead to a high salary and a fantastic career. In 1999, this was the path to take if you wanted to be successful. But he only stayed with the company for six months. He wasn't happy in his job because it didn't give him a sense of purpose in his daily life.

My brother is very creative and he's an entrepreneur at heart. He likes having the freedom to organize his day how he wants and to do his work when he feels at his best and most inspired. At twenty-five, he loved going out, partying and meet-ing girls. So he decided to create a social networking site for people like him who were into socializing. This meant he could combine what he loved doing with a less structured working day. It was very hard in the beginning, as is often the case with start-ups. But even though he didn't have any money and the future seemed bleak at times, he never gave up. His site eventu-ally became one of the top ten most visited websites in Den-mark. His company was worth a lot and ended up making a lot of money, but when Facebook arrived in Denmark his site went under within six months. No one wanted to use it anymore—they were only interested in Facebook. He sold his share in the company for one euro. So what next? People gave him lots of so-called good advice, saying things like, "Well, it's great that you followed your passion, but now it's time to grow up and get serious," or "Why don't you find a normal job like everyone else in the Internet sector?"

My brother wasn't having any of it. Ever since he was little, he'd always had health issues. He suffered from allergies and asthma and was often sick. So he decided to find a solution that would improve his health. He went to see a nutritionist, who advised him to eliminate lactose and gluten from his diet. It worked and he felt a lot better. His allergies and asthma dis-appeared. He spent months reading every book he could find on health and nutrition, and attended conferences around the world on the subject. He then decided to follow his new passion: to provide people with healthier, more natural food. In 2009, he opened his first restaurant in Copenhagen, 42 Raw, featuring a vegan menu free of animal protein and fat, lactose and gluten.

Jesper now owns three restaurants in Copenhagen, and

I am a partner in the company. He still doesn't make a lot of money—just enough to afford a nice standard of living (which in Denmark is obviously pretty good compared with the rest of the world). But he's happy and passionate about his project. His prospects are good, but in the meantime he is nevertheless doing what he wants to do in life.

COMPARISONS ARE BAD!

Let's take a look at the surveys that establish a connection between a country's wealth and the happiness of its people. The Gallup World Poll,[3] for example, shows a general relationship between the two. It's also obvious that it is hard to talk about well-being or happiness in countries where there are high levels of poverty and where people's basic human needs are not being met.

But if we look closer, the relationship between income and well-being is far from automatic. First, there is not necessarily a direct correlation between income and happiness in wealthy countries, although a nation's specific features may contribute to its people's happiness, such as democracy, a functioning legal system, the absence of war, personal freedom, and so on. Second, the increase in worldwide wealth over the past thirty years has had no effect on the level of happiness expressed by different populations. And last, when we examine each country individually, we don't always see a connection: the United States, which boasts one of the highest GDPs per capita in the world (around $57,700),[4] only ranks thirteenth in overall well-being on the World Happiness Report 2016. Costa Rica, on the other hand, is sixty-fourth in GDP per capita (with the equivalent of $10,000), but challenges the United States on the World Happiness Report, since it's fourteenth on the list! Denmark, which ranks eighth in GDP per capita, comes first in overall well-being and happiness.

Ultimately, this report demonstrates that money does influence happiness, but primarily at low income brackets. Beyond a certain threshold where people's basic human needs are met, money has very little or no effect on well-being.

Why is this? Economist Richard Layard talks of the individual's ability to adapt quickly to new situations.[5] He believes the main problem with material goods is that human beings soon grow accustomed to a new state of being. For example, if someone changes their job to earn more money, they will initially feel happier financially. But it will only last for a few weeks, because they will adapt to their new standard of living and their level of happiness will return to where it was before. The same is true for all acquisitions of material goods: we very quickly get used to a new house or a new car and our initial joy soon normalizes. Experts have observed, for instance, that the level of happiness of lottery winners tends to return to its usual level after a short-lived period of joy, whereas some winners even sink into depression. The most famous study on the subject was published in 1978 in the *Journal of Personality and Social Psychology*.[6] The results were based on interviews with lottery winners, a control group of "nonwinners" and victims of serious accidents. The lottery winners experienced a surge in happiness during the months following their good news, after which their happiness level returned to where it was before. Broadly speaking, the study showed that after a few months, the winners, nonwinners and accident victims were almost at the same level of happiness, or shall we say, well-being.

To understand the connection between money and happiness, Richard Layard proposes a theory that he calls "relative income." The principle behind relative income is simple: a rich person is anyone who earns more than their neighbor. For most people, what is important is not absolute income but income in relation to others. Layard cites the example of two imaginary situations: in the first, you earn $50,000 and other people earn $25,000. In the second, you earn $100,000 and others earn $250,000. When students at Harvard University were asked which situation they would prefer, the vast majority chose the first option.[7]

At the end of the day, the most toxic threat to our happiness is being in competition with others. In the financial sector, it's quite common for bankers who receive astronomical bonuses to be unhappy if they know that someone else received more than they did. Again, relative income blinds them to reality and makes them dissatisfied.

You don't need a PhD in economics to understand that comparisons are the quickest route to frustration—unless you are wise enough to compare yourself with people who have less than you, in which case the effect can be positive and leave you feeling luckier. Unfortunately, however, most people compare themselves with those who have more. It's a vicious cycle that's hard to escape, because once people reach their aspirational level of wealth, they simply compare themselves to new people who have even more. But let's not be naïve: it's undeniable that having money is great and that all things being equal, it offers you more freedom. The problem is that most people mistakenly think money will make them happier, whereas often it's just the start of this endless race for more. The idea that we're unhappy because we have little or no money may console us for a time and hide the real reasons for our discontent, but when the money is flowing in and we're still no happier, we no longer have any excuse for our discontent, which leads to panic. We can't help but ask ourselves, "I'm rich and I can buy whatever I want, but I'm not happy, so what's the problem?"

During a break between writing sessions I had lunch with a friend who has a very important job with a major French company. My friend is handsome, intelligent, likable and rich. He is not French but he lives in Paris, and when we met he had just bought a magnificent apartment on one of the most fashionable streets in the eighth arrondissement. He travels around the world and also has a second home in the south of France. Whenever I see him, I think, *What a great life this guy has, he's so lucky!* I started our lunch with a mundane, "So how are you?"

My question prompted a response about taxation that lasted sixty-five minutes. (Yes, I was counting!) "Well, you wouldn't believe what a nightmare it is with all the taxes I have to pay . . ."

I tried to stay positive and cheer him up. "But if you pay a lot of taxes, it's because you earn a lot, which means you can do what you want and enjoy life!"

"Yes, but I don't have the time," he replied.

I tried again: "What about your lovely home in the South? Have you been there recently?"

"Don't even talk to me about it," he replied angrily. "You can't imagine how much it's costing me in taxes and upkeep, and what's more, everyone wants to come down and visit, and then I have to entertain them!"

I decided to change the subject. "So, are you enjoying your new promotion at work?"

He looked so unhappy that for a moment I thought he was going to take it out on the poor salmon on his plate! "It's complete hell—I'm surrounded by idiots and I don't even know if I'm going to get my bonus, which is what we're all working for at the end of the day." He finished lunch by saying, "Imagine being rich and not having to worry about these sorts of problems!"

I think it's safe to say, once again, that money doesn't buy happiness.

MODESTY

I Don't Think I'm Better Than Other People

This philosophy cultivates an endearing sense
of restraint among Danes. For them, it's not
winning but taking part that counts.

n 2010, Noma in Copenhagen was voted Best Restaurant in
the World.[1] The ceremony for these prestigious awards took
place in London and Noma's chef and co-owner, René Redzepi, decided to bring his whole team with him, including dishwasher Ali Sonko. At the last minute, Sonko, who was born in
the Gambia, realized he needed a visa to enter the United Kingdom, which made it impossible for him to travel. Saddened that
they were unable to share this moment with him, the entire
Noma team arrived on stage in London wearing T-shirts embla-
zoned with Sonko's photo.

Redzepi remains very humble with regard to his success
and believes it is the result of the efforts of every member of
his team. It's all part of his philosophy: he even insists that
each chef serves the dish they have prepared to patrons. And
of course they have each tasted every dish on the menu. The
atmosphere in the staff dining room is as important as that of
the restaurant itself. The meals are prepared to the same high

standards, using the best ingredients. In 2012, Noma won the Best Restaurant in the World title for the third year in a row. This time, Ali Sonko traveled to London with the team and gave the acceptance speech. And Noma again won first prize in 2014.

BANG AND *ROLIGANS*

You don't need to dine out at Noma to capture the essence of Danish modesty (although it's a delicious experience). You could also simply read the "Law of Jante," a concept invented by Danish-Norwegian author Aksel Sandemose in 1933.[2] It is a list of ten practical rules based on a simple philosophy of modesty. For many Danes, these rules serve as a code of conduct, a little like the Ten Commandments, but focused on humility. In short, they teach you not to believe that you are better than others or to think that you have something to teach them.

This philosophy cultivates an endearing sense of restraint among Danes, but it also has its limitations: it can discourage gifted people from expressing their talents and flourishing in Danish society. It's the same issue we have already discussed in regard to education, the rejection of elitism. Sometimes you get the impression that true Danish successes happen almost by chance. You don't expect to become the best in your field because that's not the goal and people don't always react positively to it. For Danes, it's not the winning but the taking part that counts.

In the 1980s, Denmark became known around the world for its *roligans*, the supporters of Denmark's national football team. The word *"roligan"* is a pun on the English "hooligan" and *"rolig,"* which means peaceful or calm in Danish. The *roligan* spirit is based on fair play and friendliness, as opposed to violence and aggression. Enjoying yourself and having a good time are more important than winning or losing. Since the accent is on participation rather than victory, *roligans* are delighted with even the slightest success achieved by their team. They were even awarded the UNESCO Fair Play Trophy for their exemplary behavior during the Euro 1994 championship—all this while donning Viking helmets and drinking gallons of free-flowing beer.

And not just any old beer: Carlsberg, of course. "Probably the best beer in the world," as it is described in ads, with classic Danish understatement. Danish modesty can be found everywhere, even in the way we advertise products. When Carlsberg launched its ad campaign in London, the New Zealand beer brand Steinlager instantly responded with the slogan "Definitely the best beer in the world." And in the United States, Budweiser is "The king of beers." But not in Denmark, where commercials tend to focus more on products being "slightly improved" or "a bit better than usual." Danes fully appreciate and understand the meaning of these messages, whereas to a non-Dane they may suggest a lack of confidence or weakness.

Bang & Olufsen has led the audio-visual field for years. Its products are very expensive, often costing ten times more than an equivalent low-cost product. When I worked for Bang & Olufsen from 1997 to 2003, I witnessed the resistance within the group to promoting it as a luxury product. "No, it's not a luxury product, it's a quality product!" they would insist. This made the strategy in markets such as France quite complicated, where it obviously made sense to position the brand in the luxury sector. This reticence can perhaps be explained by the fact that the word "luxury" has negative connotations in

Denmark. Luxury is superfluous, superficial, ostentatious and vulgar. The term is associated with showing off and wanting to appear better than others. At the time I worked there, Bang & Olufsen held 25 percent of the market share in Denmark, an enormous figure given that their stereo systems sold for about €3,000 ($3,400). A number of my friends worked all summer long so they could afford to buy a Bang & Olufsen stereo or TV. But we never thought of it as a luxury item—absolutely not, it was a quality product! In all the years I worked for Bang & Olufsen, I don't ever remember hearing anyone claim the company was "the best," despite its market position.

THE TORTOISE AND THE HARE

When I was nineteen, having spent a year in Paris, I decided to return to Denmark to live in Copenhagen. At the time, the population of the Danish capital was around a million including the suburbs, much smaller than Paris. I wanted to take more time for myself, experience life, enjoy my freedom while I could and live relatively carefree before starting college.

I applied for a job at Café Victor, the trendiest bar in town back then and "the place to be" among Copenhagen's fashionable crowd. The bar staff looked at this young nineteen-year-old from Jutland as if I were a peasant who'd just stepped off a boat, but they ended up hiring me all the same. That's when I discovered an aspect of Denmark I wasn't familiar with: Copenhagen's supposed "elite," the bartenders took themselves very seriously and were practically local celebrities.

After a few weeks I asked them whether I could work the weekend evening shift. On Friday and Saturday evenings, Copenhagen's crème de la crème came to party. The head bartender looked at me and replied, "The weekend shift is like Formula 1, and you're a go-kart. Got it?" It was rare and surprising for me to encounter this kind of attitude in a Dane. So unusual, in fact, that a couple of weeks later the bar owner called a special meeting. He had noticed that a lot of money was going missing from the cash registers during those so-called Formula 1 nights (it's very easy to cheat in Denmark since our system is based on trust, though some would call it naïveté). The owner asked that the money be returned or else he would fire everyone. Well, everyone was fired.

The moral of the story? Even in Denmark there are people with big egos who have none of that famous Danish modesty. And whether by chance or coincidence, as with the "Formula 1" evenings, it often turns out that those who show off the most are not always the most honest, which for Danes underscores the connection between affectation and distrust.

There are some famous cases in Denmark that illustrate this theory, such as the downfall of Klaus Riskær, a brash, arrogant businessman who made a fortune in a very short period of time. After several trials, he was found guilty of fraud and sentenced to six years in prison. Same for Kurt Thorsen, a crafty property tycoon who was jailed for tax evasion. This obviously doesn't go down well in Denmark and the press usually takes it upon itself to remind everyone of the good old principles of Danish society when reporting these cases—namely, integrity and keeping a low profile.

The contrast couldn't have been greater when I got a job as a hostess at a very fashionable restaurant in Paris in 1999. The manager told us, without a shred of embarrassment, to seat the beautiful, rich people at the front of the restaurant, where they could clearly be seen, and the "ugly, common people" (to quote his awful expression) at the back, preferably by the toilets! Every so often when the front dining room was full, I would have to seat the "beautiful, rich people" in the back, too, which would always cause a huge scene. How dare I relegate them to where the "ugly, common people" sat?

"INVERTED MEGALOMANIA" AND LINE JUMPING

After the go-kart episode I immediately found another job in a nearby café that reflected my own standards and Danish values much better. The customers there were also quite selective, but no one took themselves too seriously and we were all there because the owner, Michael, was a good guy who treated us with respect and kindness. We were able to eat and drink whatever we wanted for free as long as we wrote it down in a notebook. Which everyone did, without even thinking of cheating. When it came to Danish values, all the stars were aligned: modesty goes not only with trust and honesty but with solidarity.

I finally rediscovered these values following my experience with Relais & Châteaux, which was very short and quite challenging. In 2006, I was lucky enough to be hired by the Hyatt group, an American hotel chain with an excellent corporate culture. They hired me as director of communications for Europe, Africa and the Middle East. I realize how happy it made me for nine years to be part of a group that values and respects people, and to have been surrounded by colleagues who are passionate about hotels and travel.

According to a study by researchers at Baylor University in Texas published in the *Journal of Positive Psychology* in 2012,[3] humble people are more likely than arrogant people to help others in need. In their paper, the authors explain that in thirty years of behavior research, this was the first time a link had been established between specific personality traits and a willingness to help others. "Agreeableness" also emerged as an important factor, but humility was found to be the best indicator of a person's willingness to help others. The results of the study also confirm that individual humility benefits society as a whole.

This humility may also explain a rather unexpected phenomenon in Denmark: the high consumption of antidepressants. People sometimes say to me, "If Denmark is so happy, why do Danes take so many antidepressants?" It's true: according to a 2011 study by the Danish State Serum Institute (SSI), one of Denmark's largest health research institutions, one in twelve Danes take antidepressants. Denmark is the seventh largest antidepressants consumer in the world, behind the United Kingdom, Sweden, Canada, Portugal, Australia and the sad champion Iceland.[4] But this is not necessarily because they are unhappier than inhabitants of other countries. It may simply be because, being more modest and less embarrassed about their weaknesses, they find it easier to admit they're not well and seek help. Economist Richard Layard also suggests that a significant number of cases of depression are never treated or even diagnosed.[5]

Needing to take antidepressants is not taboo in Danish society. Claus Møldrup, of the Department of Pharmaceutical Sciences at the University of Copenhagen, has analyzed this phenomenon and explains that culturally, Denmark is very accepting and understanding of depressive disorders.[6] Danes are not ashamed of talking about their depression and even less so of treating it to get better. By contrast, Møldrup observes that depression is still a very sensitive and sometimes shameful subject in many countries, particularly in southern Europe. He also points out another relevant explanation: the lack of light in Nordic countries. For nine months of the year the days are very short and night falls around 3 p.m., which can have a negative psychological effect on people.

Let's turn the question on its head for a moment. Whether or not they have hang-ups about their psychological issues, the fact remains that Danes are the seven-highest consumers of antidepressants in OECD countries.[7] What if that was making them "high"? In other words, what if it was the euphoric effect of the drugs that was making Danes the happiest people in the world? The question has already been asked, and the theory doesn't stand up to scrutiny for long. First, because antidepressants have never made anyone happy. At best, they help to stabilize depression during a particularly difficult period. And second, because consumers of antidepressants in other places do not report being particularly happy. In the United States, a series of studies by the National Health and Nutrition Examination Survey (NHANES) estimates that 11 percent of Americans ages twelve and above take antidepressants.[8] Even though France fell to seventeenth position out of twenty-eight in the OECD's 2015 rankings of antidepressant consumption,[9] an average of 150 million units of tranquilizers, antidepressants and sleeping pills are still sold in France every year.[10] However, neither the Americans nor the French rank among the happiest people in the world. On the other hand, Denmark has been among the top nations ever since happiness surveys began in 1973, while antidepressants only became available in the 1980s. As Meik Wiking, a Danish professor at the OECD Happiness Research Institute, explains,[11] "Denmark's consistent appearance at the top of the happiness rankings for the past forty years negates any explanation that points to the use of antidepressants, whose introduction has not changed Denmark's performance."

Whatever the case, this wasn't something I thought about as a teenager. One Saturday night when I was seventeen, my best friend and I decided to go clubbing. The line outside the club (a ferry in Aarhus harbor) was way too long for my liking. So I decided to go against the principles my parents had taught me and jump to the front of the line. The other two hundred or so Danes in the line immediately reacted by chanting a phrase they made up on the spot: "*Om bag i køen, ja hun skal om bag i køen!*," which means "Back of the line, she has to go to the back of the line!" I was smug in thinking that I didn't have to wait like everyone else. I wasn't proud of myself when I had to walk to the back of the line and meekly take my place. But if I'd been in another country, the crowd may have hurled much worse insults at me. In this case, the Danes expressed their discontent by simply telling me to get in line.

To make myself feel better, I chalked up my behavior to the few beers I'd had before going out, since it went completely against the grain of what I'd been taught. In Denmark you're told from a young age that you shouldn't show off or stand out too much. As a child I always heard people say that it was best to avoid the words "always," "never," "everyone" and "no one": first, because it's impolite to make such extreme assertions, and second, because it's generally very difficult to support them.

At the end of the day, the only strict assertion all Danes would probably agree on comes from Queen Margrethe II of Denmark: "We are very proud of our modesty. It is our inverted megalomania. It is highly sophisticated!"[12]

GENDER EQUALITY

I Feel Free to Choose My Role

Each person is free to choose the right role for
themselves, without worrying about
stereotypes or taboos.

When I was eight and my brother Jesper was nine, our lovely mother took the time to sit down and explain the household chores to us. One job each per day: set the table, water the flowers, vacuum the floor, clear the table, empty the dishwasher, take the trash cans out, and so on. The jobs were small, but important for teaching us about the value of work and getting each member of the family to contribute to communal living. At no point in the distribution of chores did the girl/boy question arise. My brother and I had to do exactly the same jobs.

In life in general we both had the same things, regardless of gender: the same education, the same rights, the same restrictions. When my female friends came over, we would play dolls or house. My mother had explained very clearly that I always had to let my brother join in if he wanted to. The same went for my brother when his male friends came over to play cars or cowboys and Indians. We were never treated differently because of our gender. All the same, our family model was fairly traditional, with my father working and my mother looking after us and the house.

HOUSEHUSBANDS

Growing up, I never thought about gender equality. For me it was never an issue; it was just the way things were.

In a way, you could even say that Danish society is a very feminine one, given that it's based on values generally associated with women—like solidarity, cooperation, benevolence and modesty. The most important values remain the family and the sense of social protection. Success, as we have seen, is not synonymous with financial success. It is measured by a good work–life balance, among other things.

Expressing your feelings in public is not only accepted, it's valued. Dialogue cultivates and facilitates relationships. A young French woman I work with here in Paris and whom I like a great deal often says to me, "How can you talk so openly about yourself and your feelings with people you hardly know?" It always makes me smile. In Denmark, talking like that is normal, not embarrassing or out of place. It doesn't mean you're revealing your innermost thoughts to everyone, but that you are taking a straightforward and genuine approach with the people to whom you're speaking.

This freedom to express your feelings and talk about yourself without it being seen as a sign of weakness represents fantastic progress . . . especially for men. They embrace their share of these "feminine" values naturally and are free to be a househusband, should they so wish, without it affecting their sense of masculinity. Furthermore, maternity leave is a joint matter in Denmark. In 2002, it was extended to fifty-two weeks total. Fathers have the right to take two weeks off after the birth, mothers four weeks before and fourteen weeks afterward, but the remaining thirty-two weeks can be shared freely between both parents. And contrary to many other cultures, Danish men find it normal to share the household tasks. In fact, they look after the children and the house almost as much as women do (on average just one hour less than women, compared with 4.3 hours more spent by women than men on domestic jobs in France and the United Kingdom, and five hours more in Mexico.[1] This is a point that's often forgotten: the struggle for gender equality has liberated men as much as women. Everyone is free to choose the right role for themselves, without worrying about stereotypes or taboos.

This equal relationship between men and women is instilled in Danes from childhood, when friendships between girls and boys are very natural. At school I had as many male friends as female friends. Boys and girls aren't separated, even in sports, where they are treated exactly the same. From time to time, I would beat the boys in sixty-meter (one-third mile) races. It never bothered them; they were happy for me. The absence of gender stereotypes encourages children to develop naturally and pursue what they enjoy, not what is expected of them.

One day when I was ten, four boys from my class came to my house to declare their "collective love" for me. My mother invited them in and suggested they stay for a soda. They had bought me some small gifts with a card that read "We love you." I remember feeling a bit embarrassed, but we all sat down to talk. My mother explained to them that we were still very young and that, if they really loved me, all they needed to do was be nice to me and treat me as a friend, like one of the boys. The upshot was that we all became very good friends.

Governments in many countries around the world are aware that the struggle to improve gender equality starts in childhood. In France, for example, a government report published in 2013 concluded that "sexist prejudice and stereotypes rooted in the collective subconscious are a direct source of discrimination and, for that reason, must be combated from a very young age. Gender mixing, established by law and common in everyday life, is a necessary but insufficient condition for true equality between girls and boys, and later between women and men. It must be supported by proactive efforts by the authorities, stakeholders in the education system and schools."[2] In Holland and Austria, a series of initiatives (including a program called "Girls and Technology") have been implemented to encourage girls to choose subjects and careers where they are underrepresented. In Ireland, the Department of Education and Science has instituted an obligatory strategy promoting gender equality throughout the education system.[3]

SEA, SEX AND SNOW

In Denmark there are very few taboos between men and women. At least, I don't recall a topic we weren't allowed to discuss, either as children or adults. Everyday life is simple and relatively uncomplicated. The most mundane acts—like walking down the street carrying a large package of toilet paper you've just bought—aren't in the least embarrassing for Danes. I only did that once in Paris and I'll never forget the pitying looks I got from the people I passed. Maybe it was because I'd put the rolls in a very pretty bag that was much too small!

The only thing that really makes Danes (both male and female) feel uncomfortable is, as we've already discussed, a lack of modesty. Hearing someone brag about their success makes people blush more than talking about love or sex does.

Sexuality is very natural to the Danes. It's a normal topic of conversation at dinner parties with friends, for example. It isn't an embarrassment or a sin, and women are as free as men to pursue sex exactly as they wish. Once again, the absence of gender roles and stereotypes removes any of the moral pressure imposed by social norms or religion.

A Danish girlfriend called me one day to tell me she had bumped into an ex-boyfriend of hers while having dinner with her husband. "Well, I was a bit embarrassed in front of my husband, so I just introduced him as someone I'd had sex with once," she explained.

"That must have been a bit awkward," I replied, rather surprised.

"Yes, I got the feeling he was a bit taken aback. But better to pass him off as a one-night stand than a love story!" The Danes don't have a problem with one-night stands. In fact, they rank among the highest in the world when it comes to having them.

People in Scandinavia, including Denmark, are also among the youngest in the world when they first have sexual intercourse. Icelanders start the earliest, at 15, while in Sweden, Norway and Denmark, young people first have sex at the age of 16, as do the British. The French wait until soon after their

17th birthday, a little longer than the Americans, who are 16.9 years old on average. The average Asian loses his or her virginity between 18 and 19, and Indians not until they are nearly 20.[4]

In September 2009, an online video featuring a young Danish woman looking for the father of her child went viral. Over a million people watched it in the space of a few days. She had posted it in the hope of tracking down the father. In the video, she said she had met a charming young man at the end of a drunken evening. She didn't remember his name, but had spent a fun night with him. In her arms she was holding her baby boy, August, who had been born as a result of their one-night stand. She explained that she wasn't asking for anything from him, not money or acknowledgment of paternity. She just wanted the father to be aware he had a son.

But it was all staged! The video hadn't been made and broadcast by the young woman at all, but by the Danish tourist board, VisitDenmark, to create a buzz and attract tourists. A scandal broke out, for obvious reasons. Promoting Denmark as a country where girls sleep with strangers, and unprotected at that, is clearly in poor taste. The instigators of this rather ridiculous idea reacted by saying that the goal had been to advertise the Danes' freedom to choose their own lives, including bringing a baby into the world alone without being judged by others. VisitDenmark quickly withdrew the video, however, and issued a press release acknowledging that the message could potentially be confusing. I strongly agree! Although I will admit the story kind of makes me laugh—I find it so absurd. But even so, in a way it also confirms the very relaxed attitude Danes have toward sex. That said, this whole affair caused so much controversy that the director of VisitDenmark was forced to resign soon thereafter.

In August 2013, another Danish couple made headlines about our legendary sexual freedom. After attending a football match, they decided to prolong the pleasure by making love right on the field. Unfortunately, a stadium security guard had a different idea and interrupted them unceremoniously. Unbelievable? Hardly. The Danes apparently hold the world record for couples who have made love in public.

The practice of public nudity often surprises tourists in Copenhagen. Danish women are known to go topless on the grass in Rosenborg Castle Gardens, the city's central park, during their lunch break. Danes don't have a problem with it. It's in our DNA to have an open relationship with our bodies. This probably explains the ease with which Danes go up to each other at the end of a party and say, "I really like you. Shall we have sex?" No fuss, no pretense, just an uncomplicated approach. You want to have sex, so why deprive yourselves of an enjoyable night? But don't get too excited, it doesn't work all the time, and not with everyone!

When it comes to enjoying sex, the Danes are no different from other nationalities. Researchers around the world unanimously confirm that sex and happiness go hand in hand. British economist Richard Layard rates sex as the activity that makes people the happiest,[5] while lovemaking's very high happiness potential is also corroborated by a study undertaken by psychology postgraduate Carsten Grimm of the University of Canterbury in Christchurch, New Zealand. He found that people still prefer sex to Facebook, which is good news.[6]

FAMILY MATTERS

The absence of taboos between men and women has another major impact on how society is organized. As well as giving families the liberty to distribute roles and responsibilities among their members exactly as they wish, it gives couples complete freedom to have whatever kind of nontraditional relationship scenario they want, including cohabiting with or without children, living separately and every conceivable "blended" family setup. Danes get married too, of course, although the trend has been declining since 2008, with only thirty-one thousand couples getting married in 2010, compared with a record forty-two thousand couples in 1965.[7]

In summer 2002, I went back to Denmark for the wedding of one of my dear girlfriends. It was a beautiful celebration in an idyllic spot by the sea. The atmosphere was warm and romantic and all sixty guests were happy to be sharing this wonderful moment. In keeping with tradition, the groom stood up at dinner to give a tender, moving speech. At the end, he looked into the eyes of his bride and said, "I love you. I love you with all my heart. Even when you fart in bed and think I can't smell it—well, I love you even more." I realize that for a non-Danish reader, that may seem like a really awful thing to say. But all the guests found the image perfectly normal—romantic even. That anecdote is an excellent illustration of how very natural and unpretentious men and women are with each other in Denmark. When I tell my French and American friends the story, they don't believe me. And when I insist it's true, they look at me, taken aback, and say, "Right, so how long before they got divorced?" Fortunately, I'm able to reassure them that they are still together and very happy.

However, Denmark does have one of the highest divorce rates in Europe: 2.6 per 1,000 inhabitants in 2011, compared with 2 in France, 1.7 in Poland, and 0.7 in Ireland. Eastern European countries like Latvia at 4 and Lithuania at 3.4 hold the record. Although the divorce rate in the United States is also high (3.6 per 1,000), it is on the decrease (it was 4 in the year 2000).[8]

A few months ago, one of my closest friends in Denmark called me. She hadn't been happy for quite a while as her husband had turned out to be a serial liar. With two young children, their situation was complicated, and she had battled hard for two years, trying to find a solution. "It's over," she told me. "We got divorced yesterday. A few clicks online and new life, here I come!" But in a few clicks? Yes. Since July 1, 2013, the Danish system introduced an instant online procedure that has offered couples the chance to avoid the six-month separation period normally required before divorce can be made official. It costs 900 kroner ($136) for an immediate divorce or 1,800 kroner ($270) for a divorce with a separation period. That may shock some people who think that making divorce easier will encourage more couples to split up, and it sparked a media debate in Denmark. Some divorce lawyers said "e-divorce" could lead to couples divorcing in the heat of an argument. At the same time, divorce lawyer Mette Haulund analyzed the positive aspects of the new law in an article published in the Danish daily newspaper *Berlingske*. She said the vast majority of couples that divorce are responsible adults who have already fought for a long time to try and save their marriage.[9] Most of the time, divorce comes as the last resort after many years of soul-searching. The law simply spares already distressed couples the pain of a drawn-out and complicated procedure that pours salt in an open wound.

Regardless of what people say, this new option suits Danish society very well. As we have already seen, we are taught from a very young age to be independent and responsible for our own freedom.

GENTLEWOMEN

An important side effect of this equality between men and women is that it has freed men from the duty of automatically having to pay for both himself and the woman when they go out. In Denmark, when a man asks a woman out on a date, it doesn't necessarily mean he has to pay for dinner. More often than not, the woman pays half. She sometimes even pays for exactly what she has ordered. Once I had dinner with a man (we each paid for our own meal, of course) who drove me home afterward. When we got to my front door, he asked me politely if I would give him some money toward the gas. Another time a guy picked me up to drive to the movies. As usual, I offered to pay him back for the movie ticket. He accepted gladly, but added, "Um, thanks. Except you haven't . . . hey, don't worry, this time I'll pay for the parking!" You shouldn't expect a Danish man to offer his seat to a woman either, or help her if she's carrying something heavy, or even hold the door open for her. I always forget this detail when I go back to Denmark and frequently walk straight into closing doors.

This rule applies to all social situations: men and women pay half each, whatever their income or background. I once had dinner in Paris with the crown prince of Denmark and three other Danes. We split the bill five ways.

But back to gender equality. In Denmark it is present in all spheres of society, work, civic life and politics. In 2010, 76.5 percent of Danish men and 72.4 percent of Danish women worked—a negligible difference.[10] In France, 76 percent of men work, compared with just over 67 percent of women. A gap of fifteen points, but the difference is 74 percent to 59 percent in France if we're only looking at full-time work.[11] These figures are the result of a deep-rooted civic and political philosophy. The countries of Northern Europe pioneered the right of European women to vote: Sweden as early as 1718 (but only until 1771, and then again since 1918), and Finland, Norway and Denmark granted suffrage between 1906 and 1915. Women didn't wait much longer in Britain (1918) or Germany (1919), while women's suffrage didn't come until 1931 in Spain and Turkey, and until the Liberation in 1944 in France.

In the last Danish parliamentary elections, in 2015, 37 percent of the MPs were women. Compare that with only 18 percent in the U.S. House of Representatives, 26 percent in France, 29 percent in Britain and about 10 percent each in Brazil and Japan.[12] In the 2011 elections, the Danes elected a woman prime minister for the first time—Helle Thorning-Schmidt (incumbent until 2015). She has appointed nine women ministers out of twenty-three, representing 39 percent of her government.

In business, 21 percent of board members in Denmark are women. The figure stands at 24 percent in France, 19 percent in Britain, 17 percent in Germany and 10 percent in Italy.[13] The EU average is 14.9 percent. In Norway in 2012, 42 percent of board members were women! It is worth mentioning, though, that some countries have introduced policies to boost the presence of women. In France, a law was passed in 2011 requiring that the number of women on the boards of public companies and those with a minimum of five hundred employees reach 20 percent by 2014 and 40 percent by 2017. It's the same in Norway (a pioneer on the issue), Belgium, Iceland and Italy, where the quota is 33 percent. Britain, Germany and Denmark, among others, don't have quotas. Their women board members are therefore elected as a result of circumstance and culture, not because of any kind of obligation.

Discrimination is undeniably less of an issue in Denmark, and in Scandinavia in general, than anywhere else in the world. Gender equality has become the norm. In all of my different jobs, I have never questioned whether being a woman influences my performance. When I attend meetings or conferences, it doesn't concern me that I am often the youngest person there and the only woman. Even the uncalled-for or clumsy comments that men make at times don't really affect me. I think the reason for that is my deep-rooted feeling that I am neither superior nor inferior to any other human being—male or female. In France I've had to learn how to handle business relationships with men, because it is often necessary to set clearer boundaries than elsewhere. But that being said, I've always had the impression, whether in France or anywhere else on my many travels, that I am treated with the same respect as men (with the exception of some Middle East countries, where the situation remains complicated).

The equality between men and women in Denmark creates tangible harmony in society. It gives women the opportunity to be fulfilled both in their professional career and in their private life, and gives men the freedom to invest time and energy in family life without being hung up on what others may think.

Conclusion

The sun was setting after another idyllic day in the lovely seaside house in Spain where I'd been staying with friends. It was a magical place and I'd found there the peace and inspiration I needed to write a large part of this book. I closed my laptop, feeling very happy to be experiencing such a precious moment. I slipped on a sundress and went to have an aperitif with my friends while overlooking the water. I thought to myself, *I'm so lucky! Good friends, good laughs, good food, and conversations late into the night. I'm surrounded by nature, the sun is shining, the calm is endless, and I have completely lost the notion of time. . . . I just feel so happy!* Then my cell phone rang. It was my stepmother. "Malene, you have to come back to Denmark immediately. Your father's in the hospital. He had an emergency operation and it didn't go well. He's in a coma." And just like that, in a matter of seconds, my happiness was snatched from me. I jumped on the next plane to Copenhagen, shattered by the news.

Why am I telling you this? Because having spent several years studying happiness, and not only among the Danes, the only thing that seems really clear to me is that happiness is never permanent. In fact, there is a collective fantasy about happiness that actually makes us unhappy or at least frustrated: it's the idea that happiness is some kind of permanent state. We often imagine that once we've achieved our "ideal" life, with a perfect spouse, adorable children, a stylish house, a dream career and so on, our happiness will last forever.

It's an illusion, of course. Life is constantly changing. It's unpredictable and full of surprises, both good and bad. Some situations bring pleasure, others pain. The key is to return to what I call your own foundation of well-being. This innermost foundation, which is built throughout your life, is the starting point for enjoying or surviving life's events. It's essentially this foundation that determines our long-term level of happiness. You can experience difficult times and still have a solid bedrock of happiness and, conversely, experience times of great joy even if you have a fragile bedrock. True happiness, or at least long-term well-being, isn't these extreme periods: it's the foundation to which you return.

What makes a good foundation? Above all, it's our own personal path, our choices in life and the effort we make to get to know ourselves. Nobody can do it for us.

But it's obviously more complex than that. Environment is a major factor too; it positively or negatively affects the development of a solid foundation of well-being. People say that growing up within a loving family strengthens your foundation of well-being. I agree—in my case at any rate, my family's love gave me the solid foundation I needed to be able to carve out my path to a happy, balanced life. Yet I don't believe there's a hard-and-fast rule. It's a complicated subject studied by the world's leading cognitive scientists and personal development experts. I can't claim to give the answer here, but in my opinion, the most important pillar of happiness is love. Love in all its various forms.

Besides emotional environment, one's social environment clearly plays an important role, and that's where the Danish model comes into use. What sets it apart is that it has managed to create a system that is conducive to making people happy. In fact, I'd say it is a system that encourages individuals to build a good foundation by helping them find their place in society and making them feel free and confident in life. The Danish system is the cornerstone on which solid individual foundations are built. Since the system is based on confidence, equality, a degree of realism and a sense of community and solidarity, it gives everyone the opportunity to find their own place, which is a valuable starting point for finding long-term happiness and well-being.

But Denmark's role ends with providing a conducive environment. The rest is a matter of individual responsibility, a journey we all have to make. You can easily be born in the happiest country in the world and be unhappy, and vice versa. Being born in Denmark is far from a guarantee of happiness. We have seen how Denmark, like other countries, has its fair share of unhappy people who turn to antidepressants and alcohol to cope. The Danes also have fears and ask deep questions about their lives. Perhaps you've seen some of the country's well-known films: *The Celebration* (1998) directed by Thomas Vinterberg, in which a family reveals unpleasant truths at a dinner party, or any Lars von Trier film, such as *Dancer in the Dark*, which won the Palme d'Or in Cannes in 2000, or *Melancholia* (2011). As the title suggests, this isn't filmmaking at its

most cheerful—there is darkness and unease. But let's not forget that Denmark has also produced films like *Babette's Feast* by
Gabriel Axel, which won an Academy Award in 1988. It tells the
story of Babette, the chef of a celebrated Paris restaurant, who
flees the French civil war and takes refuge in a small village in
Denmark. One day, after fifteen years of hard work, she wins the
lottery, but instead of keeping the money for herself, she uses it
to prepare a magnificent French meal for everyone. Denmark is
like every other country, like each of us, like life itself: a combi-
nation of hard times, fears, hope, joy and sharing.

A country can't make a person happy. True happiness depends
on each individual. To reiterate, a society can only give us the
best elements with which to put together a healthy foundation—
a foundation on which we can then build our own happiness. A
foundation on which we can experience joyful moments to the
fullest or withstand life's challenges.

Unlike Babette in the film, I left the "happiest country in
the world" to seek my own happiness elsewhere. I started out
on that path when I arrived in Paris at eighteen. Along with
my luggage, I brought with me the bedrock of well-being
that Danish society had given me, together with important advantages derived from the love of my parents: self-
esteem, courage and confidence. Nevertheless, as I've already
described, my early days in Paris were awful. I had to face
many difficulties in a culture that was completely foreign to
me. I thought France was the most beautiful country in the
world, but the French mentality seemed so foreign, so different from what I had known up until that point. For example,
I had the impression that the French wanted to be the best
no matter what, and that French children were much more

dependent on their parents than we were in Denmark. I was surprised to discover that people really did believe in an elite and have ambitions of greatness, and that modesty wasn't widely recognized as an essential quality. It also seemed to me that social mobility was sluggish and that the idea of equal opportunities for all was more theory than practice. Undoubtedly, France and Denmark are different cultures. We don't have the same attitudes toward taxes, work–life balance or relationships between men and women, among other things.

"If you don't agree with it, just stay in your own country!" Good point. Why did I decide to settle in France if the ideal model of happiness is in Denmark? First of all, because, as I've just said, a country won't make you happy, but what you have inside of you will. Second, because I fell in love. In love with France and its people. I love the passion the French have for life. They know better than anyone how to enjoy good food while having fascinating discussions about the meaning of life! Yes, I think they are rather individualistic, but they are endearingly complex and full of contrasts, which gives them so much depth and charm. The French have an amazing ability to find enjoyment in everything they do—even life's most banal things. I've been living in France for more than twenty years and I'm still discovering new facets of the French personality. I'm well aware that the French didn't ask me to come here and that it's certainly not up to them to adapt to my standards; it's up to me to respect this country and the people receiving me in their homeland. That's one of the reasons why I've spent a lot of time getting to know and understand this very beautiful, rich culture and learning how to speak the language.

For my own personal happiness my choice is France. But I know that my foundation of well-being is strongly linked to the values that Denmark has given me—to the ten reasons I've shared with you in this book. They all coexist in Danish culture, but I am certain you can find them, and even develop them, in any corner of the world. Even if the country where you live doesn't hand them to you on a platter like in Denmark, you can always look for them within yourself and cultivate them in your own life.

Let's look at how very different people around the world have made these ten values an essential instrument for their happiness and the happiness of others.

Trust. Muhammad Yunus, who is called "the banker to the poor," made trust his tool for transforming development economics and the daily lives of tens of thousands of people. He founded the Grameen Bank, the first micro-credit institution, in effect trusting thousands of people by giving them micro-loans without requiring collateral. The vast majority have been paid back in full, even though Bangladesh isn't highly ranked among countries where trust prevails. His work won him the Nobel Peace Prize in 2006. Trust is above all something you carry within yourself, and Yunus is one extraordinary illustration. Of course there are places and countries where you have to be more careful, but when you look people straight in the eye, trust can be established everywhere. Trust in institutions and governments is more complicated, because corruption may be involved or the situation may be more complex. To create a society built on trust, each individual must first of all put this principle into practice themselves.

Education. As we have seen, educational systems are often focused on the drive for excellence. The international education model still concentrates largely on learning by heart and scoring high, rather than children's enjoyment or desire to learn. But here again, parents can support their children on their path to personal fulfillment without forcing them to be the best or projecting their own ambitions onto them. Whenever I discuss this matter with one of my Chinese friends, she always says, "Even though school in China grooms my daughter for the elite, I am careful to ensure she finds her own way without pressure from me." Proof that the Danes aren't the only ones who focus on their child's personal fulfillment. Closer to home but further back in time, in Germany in 1919 Rudolf Steiner founded the first free Waldorf School, based on a set of innovative pedagogical theories that give as much value to artistic and manual activities as to intellectual work. With 1,039 schools, Waldorf Steiner is the largest network of independent schools in the world.

Freedom and Independence. Carving out your own path in life—by recognizing who you really are and what you like doing—is a difficult task. But if you are prepared to pay the price, it is worth freeing yourself from the life or path imposed on you by society, family or conventions. That is what Malala Yousafzai, a very courageous Pakistani girl, chose to do. She took her destiny into her own hands and fought for girls' right to education. She almost lost her life doing it when she was victim of a murder attempt by the Taliban. In 2013, she was the youngest person in history to be nominated for the Nobel Peace Prize and became the youngest laureate in 2014. It would be impossible not to mention Nelson Mandela here, too, as his personal struggle must be the most incredible and admirable in history. He devoted his life to creating a better world.

Equal Opportunities. We each have the chance to contribute to creating opportunities for other people every day. While we wait for the solution to come from "above" (whether public or private decision makers), each individual's actions can change another person's destiny. The main fields for equal opportunities are sports and entrepreneurship. Individuals are nevertheless still needed to encourage and push young people. Two-Michelin-starred French chef Thierry Marx has launched a free catering training course called "Cuisine, mode d'emploi(s)" for young people with no qualifications who come from difficult backgrounds. In the same vein, French entrepreneur Xavier Niel has founded a completely free digital technology school. His aim: to make good-quality training available to anyone talented and motivated. These initiatives bring hope and have the power to inspire all of us to help give opportunities to others.

Realistic Expectations. The Danish model shows that having realistic expectations helps us live better, but being realistic doesn't mean having no ambition. After all, Danes aspire to having meaningful lives. Do you know who said, "I always like to look on the optimistic side of life, but I am realistic enough to know that life is a complex matter"? It was Walt Disney, who created the most famous dreamworld for children (and adults). Setting yourself realistic objectives is a good start if you want to be happy. That doesn't mean you have to give up your dreams, it just means you have to be realistic about the time you need and the price you have to pay to achieve them. As American novelist and editor Edgar Watson Howe said, "Half the unhappiness in the world is due to the failure of plans which were never reasonable, and often impossible."

Solidarity. Respecting others is a personal choice. Whatever country we live in, we are all free to choose how to behave toward other people. Whether or not our social system is designed for redistribution, we are all free to share in our own way. John F. Kennedy said, "My fellow Americans, ask not what your country can do for you, ask what you can do for your country." Americans Bill and Melinda Gates are an excellent example of how this call for solidarity can be answered. In 2000, they set up the Bill and Melinda Gates Foundation with the goal of helping the world's population in the areas of health and education. They declared they would donate 95 percent of their wealth, which is estimated at $73 billion, to the Foundation. In 2010, they launched The Giving Pledge initiative, which asks the world's wealthiest individuals to donate 50 percent of their fortune to philanthropy. Warren Buffett has committed to donating 99 percent of his wealth. Of course, the remaining 1 percent is more than enough for him to live on, but it is still a brave gesture and one that few of the world's richest people are matching. Even if you don't pay as high taxes as the Danes and you don't trust your country's institutions, you have the personal freedom to show solidarity toward those around you, within your own capabilities.

Work–Life Balance. This is also something each person can choose—it wasn't invented by the Danes! British entrepreneur

Richard Branson, for example, is known for valuing the role of his family and making them his priority in life. His advice to people who have to compromise with very demanding careers is simply to leave space in their schedule for family time. The companies that understand the importance of creating a balance between career and private life will, in my opinion, attract tomorrow's most talented people. Happy employees are the most efficient and loyal. Having a career in a company that doesn't even consider this aspect remains a personal choice. To an extent, we can all choose a job or company that offers a work–life balance, regardless of the country or system in which we live.

Money. This issue is inextricably linked to the preceding one, and once again, you don't need to be in Denmark to have other priorities in life. I was moved by the example of Tom Crist, a retired Canadian who won a $40 million jackpot in the 2013 lottery. He decided to donate all his winnings to charity, in particular a cancer research foundation, in memory of his wife, whom he had lost to cancer two years earlier. "I was fortunate enough in my career to set myself up and my kids anyway, and there was no doubt in my mind where that money was going to go, it was going to go to charity." Well said.

Modesty. This isn't the easiest category to find examples for, because modest people don't like being talked about; they prefer to discreetly focus on the important things. François Michelin, former boss of the famous French tire company, never liked giving interviews or being the subject of conversation. Yet, as the head of one of the best-known companies in the world, responsible for keeping Airbus and Rolls-Royce moving, he certainly had plenty to brag about. Zinedine Zidane is another example of an unquestionably talented and internationally recognized man who has managed to remain very modest. "Individual performance is not the most important thing. You win and lose as a team," he has said. The happiest people often demonstrate a degree of humility toward life, as do those who are committed to helping others, like Mahatma Gandhi. Fighting on behalf of others is a form of humility toward oneself and life.

Gender Equality. This is something people have to battle for all over the world. In China, Guo Jianmei has dedicated her life to defending the rights of women. Thanks to her support, Chinese women are daring to assert their place in society. In France, Bulgarian-born French philosopher Julia Kristeva launched the Simone de Beauvoir Prize for Women's Freedom to mark the centennial of the French writer and philosopher's birth; the prize is awarded in recognition of outstanding work to promote freedom and equality for women around the world. The honorees often fight grueling battles against very complicated systems, but they understand that the happiness of millions of people is at stake.

I could give many more examples of extraordinary people— forgotten or famous, here or on the other side of the world—who, in their own way, fight to defend or are committed to supporting these ten pillars of happiness in order to give other people the best chance of building a solid foundation for their well-being.

During my travels around the world, I've been fortunate enough to encounter cultures and people who have enabled me to put my own foundation and reference points into perspective. I've realized how lucky I was to be born in Denmark and to grow up with the values I've shared with you in this book. But I've also realized that the most important thing behind these ten pillars (and which sums them all up) is the freedom to be true to yourself. Albert Camus beautifully said, "But what is happiness except the simple harmony between a man and the life he leads?" I think we would all do well to keep his words within each of us.

Knowing who you are requires time and effort, so I'd like to share with you some very simple "life philosophies" that I've collected on my journey. They improve my life by increasing my well-being and moments of happiness, and I am sure you are already familiar with some of them.

1. I Am My Own Best Friend. The only person you are certain of spending time with (lots of time) throughout your life is yourself. So we have a vested interest in getting along with ourselves, otherwise our journey through life could be very long and hard. By listening to yourself, getting to know yourself and taking care of yourself, you solidify the foundation for a happy life. Long-term well-being and happiness begins with self-knowledge. As Gandhi very neatly put it, "The greatest traveller is not the one who has explored the world ten times, but the one who has explored himself just once."

2. I Don't Compare Myself to Others. The surest source of unhappiness is comparison—running the rat race will never make you satisfied. All in the name of having more than other people. The only exception that has the potential to make you feel positive is comparing yourself with those who have less. Not to think of yourself as superior, of course, but to be aware of how lucky you are! As the great French philosopher Voltaire wrote in his moral poem "La Bégueule" in 1772, "Perfect is the enemy of good."

3. I Ignore Society's Standards and Pressures. The freer we feel to do things in the order that suits us and in our own way, the more likely we are to be in tune with ourselves and ultimately to live the life we want, not the one expected of us.

4. I Always Have a Plan B. When you feel like you only have one choice in life, you are frightened of losing what you have. Fear often means we make the wrong decisions for the wrong reasons. By having potential alternatives, we are more likely to have the courage to deal with any difficulties thrown at us by Plan A in a way that remains true to ourselves.

5. I Choose My Battles. In life, we face battles, big and small, every day. It would be impossible for us to rise to all of them. It is crucial that we choose our battles wisely—namely, the ones that will actually benefit us. As for the others, you're better off learning to let them go, like water off a duck's back.

6. I Am Honest with Myself and I Accept the Truth. The more realistic and honest we are about the truth in a given situation, the more likely we are to find the right solution to change it. However difficult it may be, if the starting point is based on truth and we accept that truth, we are better able to see the things we can't change and focus instead on the things we can.

Right diagnosis, right treatment. Proper solutions are impossible if the starting point is a lie.

7. I Cultivate Realistic Idealism. It's vital to have big plans that give meaning to our lives . . . while keeping our expectations realistic. The same goes for our relationships. The more realistic our expectations of others, the more likely we are to be pleasantly surprised in life.

8. I Live in the Present. Living in the present means enjoy the journey itself without fantasizing about the destination or regretting the departure point. I keep in mind something someone very special once told me: "The point is the journey, not the destination." Although it is important to have a plan to guide you, happiness is rarely waiting for you when you arrive. You will find it along the way, in the here and now, as you move forward in the journey of life.

9. I Give Myself Several Sources of Well-Being. Or, in the words of that old proverb, I don't put all my eggs in one basket. Being dependent on a single source of happiness—work, a loved one, and so on—is risky because it is fragile. Work every day at establishing a balanced mix of sources, people and activities that make you happy. For me, one very important source of happiness is laughter—it gives me an almost instant feeling of well-being.

10. I Love Others. Love, sharing and generosity are the most wonderful sources of happiness, in my opinion. Since sharing and giving make one feel happy, they help build a solid, long-term foundation for well-being. Albert Schweitzer, the 1952 Nobel Peace Prize winner, knew what he was talking about when he said, "Happiness is the only thing that doubles when you share it."

One last thing before we continue on our journey toward, I hope, happiness. Strangely enough, I wrote the book you are holding in your hands during a difficult time in my life. But as I finish it, I realize I feel profoundly happy to have shared so many of the thoughts and adventures that are important to me. Not a paradox, just happiness's last little wink at us. Whatever ordeals life throws at you, staying true to yourself and sharing (like through writing, along with sincerity and openness) are, to my mind, the best ways of tapping into your foundation of well-being. With the support of this foundation, Danish-made or not, life sometimes lets us achieve our dreams. Remember that nine-year-old girl whose wish was to become the ambassador of Denmark? Well, if this books manages to spread some positive thoughts about my country to the rest of the world, then I'll have fulfilled my dream.

Acknowledgments

Thank you to my parents for the precious foundation of love, trust, and freedom that they've given me to follow my dreams and create a meaningful life with purpose. Thank you to my brother, Jesper, for his unwavering support, frankness, inspiration, and compassion. Thank you to all my dear friends for being there for me, and for their warm encouragements throughout this adventure. A special thank you to my friend Jeffrey Rosen for his guidance and support. Thank you to wonderful Mathilde Oliveau, who was by my side in the process to offer her critical and inspiring insights, always with great kindness. Thank you to my agent, Susanna Lea, for her invaluable advice and positive energy and to her fantastic team for their support. Thank you to Jill Bialosky and Maria Rogers at Norton for their engagement and enthusiasm.

Notes

INTRODUCTION

1. Danish political drama series.
2. Skat.dk, the Danish tax authority's website.
3. Richard Layard, *Happiness: Lessons from a New Science* (New York: Penguin Press, 2005).
4. David Lykken and Auke Tellegen, "Happiness Is a Stochastic Phenomenon," *Psychological Science* 7 (1996).
5. Thierry Janssen, *Le défi positif: Une autre manière de parler du bonheur et de la bonne santé* (Les liens qui libèrent, 2011).
6. http://www.grossnationalhappiness.com/wp-content/uploads/2012/04/Short-GNH-Index-edited.pdf
7. Donella H. Meadows et al., *The Limits to Growth* (Universe Books, 1972).
8. http://www.happinessresearchinstitute.com/profiler/4578771590

CHAPTER 1: TRUST

1. Gert Tinggaard Svendsen, *Tillid* (Tænkepauser, 2012).
2. Ranking based on research undertaken by Svendsen in 2005 and the results of World Values Surveys.
3. Yann Algan and Pierre Cahuc, *La Société de défiance, comment le modèle français s'autodétruit* (CEPREMAP collection, Éditions Rue d'Ulm, 2007).

4.   *European Social Survey*, 2010.

5.   http://www.forbes.com/pictures/eglg45ehhje/no-1-denmark/

6.   *World Justice Project*, 2015.

7.   UNSDSN, *World Happiness Report 2013*.

8.   Pierre Cahuc and Yann Algan, *Peut-on construire une société de confiance en France?* (Éditions Michel Albin, 2009).

9.   Christian Bjørnskov, *Det er et lykkeligt land* [literally, *It's a Happy Country*] (Copenhagen, Denmark: The Happiness Institute, September 2013).

10. *Reader's Digest* "Lost Wallet Test" (2001).

11. *Børsen* and Copenhagen Business School, *Tillid* conference (August 2012).

12. Stephen M. R. Covey, *The Speed of Trust: The One Thing That Changes Everything* (First Editions, 2008).

13. http://www.leadershipnow.com/CoveyOnTrust.html

14. Rambøll Management/Analyse Danmark for *Jyllands-Posten* (2009).

15. Poul Nyrup Rasmussen in his speech on Danish Constitution Day in Copenhagen (June 5, 1999).

16. Transparency International, *Global Corruption Report 2013* (July 2013).

17. Transparency International, *Perception Corruption Index, 2013, 2014 and 2015*.

18. World Values Surveys, 1980–2000.

CHAPTER 2: EDUCATION

1.   The Statens Uddannelsesstøtte [State Education Grant] is 5,700 kroner ($870) gross per month for a student not living with their parents.

2.   http://www.oecd.org/edu/ceri/

3.   UNESCO, *Revisiting Lifelong Learning for the 21st Century* (2001), http://www.unesco.org/education/uie/publications/uiestud28.shtml

4.   Interview with Emma Rytter Hansen (age nineteen) conducted by the author on November 1, 2013.

5.   Danish Ministry of Culture, 2012, http://www.dst.dk/pukora/epub/Nyt/2014/NR157.pdf

6.   http://www.dr.dk/tv/program/9-z-mod-kina/

7.   In the OECD PISA 2010 survey, students in Hong Kong and Shanghai had the highest results of all the OECD countries assessed.

8. OECD PISA 2012 survey, http://www.oecd.org/pisa/keyfindings/pisa-2012-results.htm

9. Seventy-one percent of French secondary schoolchildren say they are bored at school, according to a survey among 760 children carried out in 2010 by AFEV (Association de la Fondation Étudiante pour la Ville, an educational support organization).

10. OECD, *Student Engagement at School 2000*.

11. *Berlingske* (January 8, 2007).

12. *Politiken* (May 7, 2009).

13. *Politiken* (December 20, 2012).

14. https://www.service-public.fr/particuliers/vosdroits/F12215

15. German Ministry for Education, 2015, http://www.datenportal.bmbf.de/portal/en/brochure.html

16. OECD, *Education at a Glance 2011*.

17. http://www.bbc.com/news/education-11677862

18. College Board (not-for-profit organization), *Trends in College Pricing 2014–2015*.

19. Fondation pour l'Innovation Politique, *Young People Facing the Future: An International Survey* (2008).

20. http://europa.eu/epic/countries/denmark/index_en.htm

21. Fondation pour l'Innovation Politique, ibid.

22. OECD PISA 2012, ibid.

23. Denmark ranks just above the average of the OECD countries in reading comprehension and performs very highly in math, OECD PISA 2010.

24. Interview at Skaade Skole in Aarhus conducted by the author in August 2013.

25. Tal Ben-Shahar, *Happier: Can You Learn to Be Happy?* (McGraw-Hill Professional, 2008).

26. AFEV, ibid.

27. Yale Center for Emotional Intelligence, Born This Way Foundation (founded by singer Lady Gaga) and Robert Wood Johnson Foundation, 2015, http://ei.yale.edu/what-we-do/emotion-revolution/

28. Horace Mann League, *School Performance: The Iceberg Effect*, 2015.

CHAPTER 3: FREEDOM AND INDEPENDENCE

1. Conseil Économique et Social [French Economic and Social Council], *Le travail des étudiants* (2007); L'OVE [French National Observatory of Student Life], «Les étudiants et leurs conditions de vie en Europe,» *OVE Infos* no. 13 (2005).
2. http://www.marketwatch.com/story/nearly-4-out-of-5-students-work-2013-08-07
3. Center for Ungdomsforskning, http://www.cefu.dk/service/english.aspx
4. "Christiana enfin libre," *Courrier International* (June 23, 2011).
5. http://epp.eurostat.ec.europa.eu/cache/ITY_OFFPUB/KS-SF-10-050/EN/KS-SF-10-050-EN.PDF
6. *Forbes*, 2013, http://www.forbes.com/sites/trulia/2013/07/23/kids-arent-moving-out-yet/#5c63bcbb6eb1
7. http://www.ncbi.nlm.nih.gov/pmc/articles/PMC3367275/
8. Report by the *Journal of Economic Behavior and Organization* (2011).
9. OECD, *Education at a Glance 2009*.
10. UNDP, *Human Development Report*, 2009.
11. Council of Europe, *Draft Report on Fostering Social Mobility as a Contribution to Social Cohesion* (2011).

CHAPTER 4: EQUAL OPPORTUNITY

1. OECD, "A Family Affair: Intergenerational Social Mobility across OECD Countries," in *Economic Policy Reforms: Going for Growth* (March 2010).
2. The curve was introduced in a 2012 speech by Alan Krueger, the chairman of the Council of Economic Advisers. The name was coined by former CEA staff economist Judd Cramer.
3. Danish Ministry of Education, 2012.
4. Statistics Denmark (2011).
5. Author's interview with a partner in a Copenhagen law firm who preferred to remain anonymous (November 11, 2013).

CHAPTER 5: REALISTIC EXPECTATIONS

1. Max Weber, *Die protestantische Ethik und der Geist des Kapitalismus* (1904–05), translated into English by Talcott Parsons in 1930.
2. OECD, *Better Life Index 2016*.
3. Kaare Christensen, Anne Marie Herskind, and James W. Vaupel, "Why Danes Are Smug: Comparative Study of Life Satisfaction in the European Union," *BMJ* (October 2006).
4. Tal Ben-Shahar, *Happier: Can You Learn to Be Happy?* (McGraw-Hill Professional, 2008).
5. Sylvie Tenenbaum, *C'est encore loin le bonheur?* (InterEditions, 2007).

CHAPTER 6: SOLIDARITY AND RESPECT FOR OTHERS

1. United States Holocaust Memorial Museum.
2. http://www.yadvashem.org/yv/en/righteous/statistics.asp
3. YouGov survey for Ugebrevet A4 (2012).
4. Statistics Denmark, 2013.
5. OECD (February 2016).
6. Statistics Denmark, 2013.
7. Survey by Greens Analyseinstitut for *Børsen* (2010).
8. Ipsos Public Affairs poll published in *Le Monde*, BFM TV and the *Revue française des finances publiques* [French Public Finance Review] (October 14, 2013).
9. Centro de Investigaciones Sociológicas (CIS) annual survey (November 2013).
10. http://www.irs.gov/Individuals/International-Taxpayers/U.S.-Citizens-and-Resident-Aliens-Abroad
11. https://www.federalregister.gov/quarterly-publication-of-individuals-who-have-chosen-to-expatriate
12. Ugebrevet A4 survey, 2011, http://www.ugebreveta4.dk/undersoegelser/aspx
13. Analyse Danmark survey for Ugebrevet A4 (2012).
14. Ugebrevet A4 (August 12, 2013), http://www.ugebreveta4.dk/ledige-skal-bevise-at-de-soeger-job_14047.aspx
15. OECD, Eurostat, MISSOC, LeFigaro.fr (February 2012).
16. http://en.wikipedia.org/wiki/Unemployment_benefits#Unemployment_Benefits_in_the_United_States

17.   OECD, "Long-Term Unemployment (12 Months and Over)" (July 16, 2013), http://www.oecd-ilibrary.org/employment/long-term-unemployment-12-months-and-over_20752342-table3

18.   http://www.idea.int/vt/countryview.cfm?id=63 and OECD, *Better Life Index 2016*.

19.   http://www.oecdbetterlifeindex.org/countries/denmark/

CHAPTER 7: WORK–LIFE BALANCE

1.   OECD, *Better Life Index*, "Work–Life Balance," http://www.oecdbetter lifeindex.org/topics/work-life-balance/

2.   Statistics Denmark (2013).

3.   Lederne survey (October 2012).

4.   OECD, "How's Life? Measuring Well-Being" report (2011).

5.   DTU Transport (Danish Department of Transport) report (2012).

6.   Denmark.dk.

7.   Jeppe Trolle Linnet, *Politiken* (November 10, 2013).

8.   European School Survey Project on Alcohol and Other Drugs, *The 2011 ESPAD Report*, http://www.espad.org/Uploads/ESPAD_reports/2011/The_2011_ESPAD_Report_SUMMARY.pdf

9.   *National Survey on Drug Use and Health: Summary of National Findings* (2011). Report jointly prepared by the Center for Behavioral Health Statistics and Quality (CBHSQ), Substance Abuse and Mental Health Services Administration (SAMHSA), U.S. Department of Health and Human Services (HHS) and RTI International.

10.   http://fr.ria.ru/russia/20101006/187570014.html

11.   INPES (2008), http://www.inpes.sante.fr/slh/articles/398/02.htm

12.   European Social Survey (2010).

13.   Megafon survey for *Politiken* (December 2011).

14.   SFI—Det Nationale Forskningscenter for Velfaerd [Study on the voluntary sector in Denmark] (2006).

15.   European Quality of Life Survey: Participation in Volunteering and Unpaid Work (2011).

16.   Corporation for National and Community Service, "United We Serve" (2010).

CHAPTER 8: RELATIONSHIP TO MONEY

1. *What If Money Was No Object?* Alan Watts, https://www.youtube.com/watch?v=khOaAHK7efc

2. Søren Kierkegaard, *Journals 1A* (1835). English translations from Søren Kierkegaard, *Papers and Journals: A Selection*, trans. Alastair Hannay (New York: Penguin, 1996).

3. Gallup World Poll (2010), http://www.gallup.com/strategicconsulting/en-us/worldpoll.aspx?ref=f

4. http://en.wikipedia.org/wiki/List_of_countries_by_GDP_%28PPP%29_per_capita

5. Richard Layard, *Happiness: Lessons from a New Science* (New York: Penguin Press, 2005).

6. Philip Brickman, Dan Coates, and Ronnie Janoff-Bulman, "Lottery Winners and Accident Victims: Is Happiness Relative?" *Journal of Personality and Social Psychology* (1978).

7. This experiment comes from Sara J. Solnick and David Hemenway, "Is More Always better?: A Survey on Positional Concerns," *Journal of Economic Behavior and Organization* 37, no. 3 (1998), 373–383.

CHAPTER 9: MODESTY

1. The S. Pellegrino World's 50 Best Restaurants list is published annually by *Restaurant* magazine. Noma has won the Best Restaurant in the World award four times to date, in 2010, 2011, 2012 and 2014.

2. Aksel Sandemose, *En flyktning krysser sitt spor* [A Fugitive Crosses His Tracks] (1933).

3. Jordan Labouff et al., "Humble Persons Are More Helpful Than Less Humble Persons: Evidence from Three Studies," *Journal of Positive Psychology* 7, no. 1 (2012): 16–29.

4. OECD, *Health at a Glance 2015*.

5. Richard Layard, *Happiness: Lessons from a New Science* (New York: Penguin Press, 2005).

6. Claus Møldrup, "Danskerne æder lykkepiller som aldrig før" [Danes Are Eating Antidepressants Like Never Before), *Ugebrevet A4* (December 2007).

7.   OECD, ibid.

8.   National Health and Nutrition Examination Survey (2005–08).

9.   OECD, ibid.

10. L'Assurance-Maladie, the French national state health insurance.

11. Meik Wiking, "Er Danmark dopet I lykkemålinger" [Has Denmark Been
     Doped in the Happiness Surveys?), *Jyllands-Posten* (May 27, 2013).

12. Queen Margrethe II of Denmark's New Year's speech as quoted in Helle
     Askgaard, "Denmark and the Danes," in Danish Cultural Institute, *Discover
     Denmark: On Denmark and the Danes—Past, Present and Future* (Systime, 1992).

CHAPTER 10: GENDER EQUALITY

1.   OECD, "Gender Equality Unpaid Work" (2012).

2.   http://femmes.gouv.fr/wp-content/uploads/2013/03/chiffres-
     cles-2012.pdf

3.   Eurydice for the European Commission, "Gender Differences in Educa-
     tional Outcomes: Study on the Measures Taken and the Current Situa-
     tion in Europe" (2010).

4.   Durex Global Sex Survey, 2005.

5.   Richard Layard, *Happiness: Lessons from a New Science* (New York: Pen-
     guin Press, 2005).

6.   Carsten Grimm, "*Well-Being in Its Natural Habitat: Orientations to Happi-
     ness and the Experience of Everyday Activities*," Department of Psychology,
     University of Canterbury, New Zealand (2012).

7.   Statistics Denmark, Report on Gender Equality (2011).

8.   CDC/NCHS National Vital Statistics System.

9.   *Berlingske* (July 1, 2013).

10. Statistics Denmark (2011).

11. http://www.insee.fr/fr/ffc/ipweb/ip1462/ip1462.pdf

12. Insee (2013), http://www.insee.fr/fr/themes/tableau.asp?reg_id=98&ref_
     id=CMPTEF05530

13. Ernst and Young, "Panorama 2013 des pratiques de gouvernance des
     sociétés cotées," (October 2013).